I0016419

Lives on the Line

Voices for CHANGE
from the Thailand-Burma Border

BURMA LINK

BURMA LINK

To

....

....

....

....

From

....

Lives on the Line

Voices for CHANGE
from the Thailand-Burma Border

BURMA LINK

Copyright © 2016 by Burma Link

All rights reserved.

First printing : February 2016.

ISBN　　　 : 978-952-68283-3-6 (paperback)

ISBN　　　 : 978-952-68283-2-9 (EPUB)

Author　　 : Burma Link

Publisher　 : Burma Link

Cover images : Burma Link, Eugene, Feliz Solomon,

　　　　　　　　Naga National Council, Saw Mra Raza Linn

BURMA LINK is a non-profit organisation that was founded in 2012 in Mae La refugee camp in Thailand to help the people of Burma reach out to the world and have their voices heard. Burma Link is made up of people from Burma and around the world who share an unwavering belief that at this critical time of change, upholding the voices of all Burma's people is more important than ever. We especially advocate for Burma's long-silenced ethnic nationalities and displaced people, and share their voices and stories with local and international audiences.

For more information, please visit
www.burmalink.org

For full versions of some stories in this book,
and many other Voices for Change, please visit
www.burmalink.org/voices

Contents

Foreword

There are no words for what this book, these stories, and the people behind them, mean to me. These stories have no less than changed my life, and if you give them a chance, they might change yours too. Sharing these stories and helping Burma's silenced voices be heard is not my job, it never was - it has become my personal mission. And I know in my heart that these stories can inspire the people of Burma to take action and change the direction of their country. They could also inspire you to change your life or to reach out to others. But don't take my word for it, just read the book and see how you feel.

A few years ago I never would have believed it if you told me what I do today, but as we all know, life rarely turns out the way we plan. For me, everything changed when I came to the Thailand-Burma border in 2011. I was instantly amazed by the courage and spirit of the people of Burma who live on the border and who have almost none of those things that I had grown up to take for granted – things like human rights and freedom. Unbelievably, I found them the most grateful, giving, determined, and inspiring people I had ever met. I couldn't believe the injustice, and felt that I had no choice but to stay and do what I could to help.

I was living in Mae La refugee camp - the largest of the nine camps along the Thailand-Burma border - when I realised that the voices and stories of the people along the border were not getting the audience and the attention they deserved. I felt a strong desire to change this, and thus got together with refugees to found an organisation called Burma Link. Soon after, we started collecting stories of refugees, women activists, migrant students, jungle medics, ethnic leaders, and freedom fighters, to share their voices with both local and international audiences.

The stories we have collected are of real-life people who have lived through extraordinary lives and struggles but never given up. Many of the stories selected for this book are prime examples of how difficulties can be overcome and often turned into success, and how determination and perseverance are stronger than any forces trying to stop them. These are stories of those who have lived through one of the longest ongoing conflicts in the world but who stand for peace, and of those who desire change for their homeland. These are Burma's *"voices for change."*

I ask you to read these Voices for Change with an open heart and an open mind. Let them move you, shock you, upset you, and amaze you. Even if these stories will inspire one person to change their life direction, to find hope, to sympathise, to stand up against injustice, to speak up against oppression and discrimination, or to fight for the long overdue rights and freedom of the people of Burma, or any another nation, then we have succeeded. That person can be you, and countless others. And for change, there is never a time like now.

Leena

Co-Founder of BURMA LINK

x   x   x

Atun Foreword

In 2012, I was one of the tens of thousands of refugees living in limbo in Mae La refugee camp in Thailand. When I met Leena and got the opportunity to get involved in helping to share the voices and stories of my people, I jumped at the chance. But even then, I never could have imagined how much there was to learn about my own people, the history, and the struggles. Indeed, these stories and the people behind them have been a source of great knowledge and remarkable inspiration for me ever since.

This book is all about stories and life experiences of people from Burma from a variety of ethnic groups and backgrounds, and how they have sacrificed their lives and been oppressed living under the military government. These are real life stories, in the voice of the people themselves, and I am so excited that they can be finally brought to a larger audience. Although I am ethnic Karen myself, these stories have opened my mind to the struggles of not only other ethnic people from Burma but even the Karen. I have also been amazed at how much we all share, regardless of where in Burma we come from or what ethnic group we belong to.

When I helped to collect these stories, it was as though everything I heard was new at first, and I realised how I had been brainwashed by the government. What I knew when I was in Burma and what I know now are two different realities. I feel so privileged to have had the chance to learn and know about my country and so many historical events directly from the people. I hope that these stories can help everyone learn more about our country, the lives of ethnic people around Burma, and the real situation on the ground. Although these stories are just a handful, they do represent the incredible struggles of so many others.

We all have our own story. I hope this book will inspire you to share your story with others as well as to really listen when someone gives you the honor and shares their story with you. If you are anything like me, this book may even inspire you to stand for the truth and work for justice, where ever that may be. Either way, I am sure that if you listen with an open heart, you will learn something very valuable for your life from the stories of these people.

Atun
Co-Founder of BURMA LINK

x   x   x

Background

Burma has experienced one of the biggest humanitarian crisis and most protracted refugee situations in the world. Millions of people from Burma, mostly ethnic nationalities in the country's borderlands, have fled armed conflicts and Burmese military run war crimes and human rights abuses that have spanned over several decades. Despite recent changes in Burma's political landscape, abuse continues in ethnic areas.

The civil war in Burma that started with the Karen armed opposition in 1949, following a failure to reach a political agreement, has been dubbed as the longest ongoing conflict in the world. The Burma Army, in order to defeat ethnic armed opposition, has targeted their military campaigns against ethnic civilians. The result has been ongoing persecution of ethnic villagers and destruction of more than 3,500 ethnic villages. As the government has exerted repressive military control over the resource rich ethnic borderlands all over the country, ethnic armies have fought to protect their lands and their people, and ethnic civilians have suffered the consequences.

The voices of Burma's ethnic nationalities have been silenced and suppressed for over 60 years, and largely remain unheard inside Burma. The education system promotes the government's views and discourages critical thinking. Few have developed an understanding of the reasons for the conflict and its human consequences, and many have adopted the government-pushed view that ethnic armies are waging a war to tear the country apart. Meanwhile, ethnic nationalities have endured killings, beatings, torture, forced labour, forced relocations, and the use of rape as a weapon of war, all committed in a culture of impunity.

The recent changes in Burma's political landscape and ceasefires signed between the Burma Army and some prominent ethnic resistance groups have given a misleading image that peace is within reach. Meanwhile, large scale offensives in northern Burma and increasing militarisation in ceasefire areas have called into question U Thein Sein's government's commitment to peace. Initial ceasefires have proven to be fragile and regularly breached, inclusive political dialogue is yet to begin, and Burma is still far from achieving a country-wide nationwide ceasefire agreement (NCA). Until there are solutions to the political goals of ethnic resistance groups that address the root causes of the conflict, there will be no peace or freedom for the ethnic people of Burma.

Over the years, at least three million people have fled Burma, whilst more than 600,000 remain internally displaced, most of them in eastern Burma. Hundreds of thousands have fled conflict and persecution to neighbouring Thailand, where more than 100,000 refugees still reside in nine official refugee camps. In addition, thousands of majority Burman civilians, usually due to their involvement in the political pro-democracy struggle, have crossed the border to flee from the repressive government. The Thailand-Burma border, during the past decades, has become home not only to scores of exiles who have fled their home for numerous reasons, but also to a highly organised movement that continues to work towards a free, peaceful, and democratic Burma.

Whilst NLD's landslide victory in the November 8 election gives much hope for change, the constitution guarantees that the Burmese military still has ultimate power, and the military's offensives and human rights violations in ethnic areas can carry on with impunity. For countless of ethnic civilians in exile and in Burma's borderlands, peace process is a priority and constitutional change a necessity.

X   X   X

" I Am Going to Bring Them to Court Some Day FOR JUSTICE "

Former Teenage Political Prisoner *Soe Lwin*

Soe Lwin is a 34-year-old man from Dawei who comes from a family of political prisoners. Despite his young age, Soe Lwin has spent nearly half of his life in prison. In 1994, Soe Lwin and 14 of his friends were arrested for distributing pamphlets asking for better education. The young teenagers, 13 and 14 years old at the time, were taken to an interrogation centre where they were brutally beaten and tortured for a period of one month, leaving one of them dead and the others in such a bad shape even prisons refused to accept them. After being medically treated with their own money, Soe Lwin and other survivors were taken to court where they were read out their sentences from a pre-written piece of paper - 14 years in prison. It was only when Soe Lwin was taken to the infamous Insein Prison that he found out he'd been given another 10-year sentence without his knowledge. Soe Lwin had to go through unspeakable atrocities in prison, from having no one to talk to but ants and geckos for three years, to being forced to survive on eating nothing but [rice] glue for weeks. At the age of 29, having spent his entire youth behind bars, Soe Lwin was finally released. Although he "lost everything" to the military regime, Soe Lwin says he has no regrets about what they did all those years ago - it was the right thing to do.

Family of political prisoners:
"We were kids. We weren't murderers"

When I was growing up, we did not have much money. My father did politics [as a member of NLD – National League for Democracy]. In 1990 national elections, the first ten people were arrested. My father was one of them. He was imprisoned for three years. Since then, he has been active in politics. I was in grade four [at the time]. Around eight or nine years old.

About a little over a year after my father was imprisoned, my mother was also arrested. I am not really sure for what reason. They [people] say, she got arrested because she sang a song and explained its meaning in her class to her students. They came and arrested her in the morning. It's a song from the student movement. [She was sentenced for] two years. She served for 1 year and 9 months.

After my mother was released, I was imprisoned. After my father was released, my mother was imprisoned. My mother was released, and I was imprisoned for my political activities.

I was between 13 and 14 years old. I was arrested on April 24, 1994, after I finished my 8 standard examinations. I had [already] been arrested before examinations, but I was released to take the examinations, then, after my exams were done, they put me back to prison.

My case was like what's happening today. There was a group of us students. We opposed tuition classes. We demanded more careful teaching at school. We collected signatures from people and distributed letters to support us. We went on the streets handing out pamphlets. And we got arrested. There were 15 of us.

We were kids. We weren't murderers. I was only fourteen. They can't put kids in prison. We were kids just handing sheets of papers like others were doing. We weren't murderers or bad kids or doing drugs or stealing. We were good kids going to school. We were just asking to teach us right.

Interrogation: "There were worms and dead ants. But we had no choice. We drank it"

The MI (Military Intelligence) said, *'They are just kids and it will not take long,'* and that they just have a few questions to ask. But my father did not listen to the MI. He put some clothes, a mosquito net, and blankets for me in the car. As soon as I got into the car, they blindfolded me and handcuffed me. Then, they took me away to the interrogation center.

For the first few days, they left us with easy questions. But on the fourth day, they put each of us in separate individual rooms. Girls and boys were separated. And that was when they started beating, kicking, and hitting us. [There were] 15 of us.

Then… At one night, I was awoken by them at around, I thought, 2 am in the morning. I got up. They blindfolded me. I thought we walked for about an hour. I could not see a thing. They sat me at a place I could not see. Then, they asked me the following questions: 'Would you like to continue attending school?' 'Tell us the truth.' 'Does your father do politics?' I told them 'I don't know.' I kept saying 'I don't know.'

It came to me the next night. I was blindfolded and they took me to that place. They kept asking the same questions. Then, that was when they started hitting me. I was blindfolded, so, I could not see a thing. They kept hitting me. I kept saying 'I don't know. I don't know.' It was in the early morning that night that they took me back to my cell. I knew they were interrogating others as well.

They came and took me away like the past nights again and again. It was on the eighth day, I think, I am not sure, I don't quite remember now anymore, that they stopped giving me water. They interrogated us, but they could not get any information, so they stopped giving us water.

We had to drink the bathroom water, the water that is used to clean the toilet in the restroom. The toilet water was in a clay pot. In the water pot, there were worms and dead ants. But we had no choice. We drank it.

They did not know we were drinking water from the toilet at first. Within a day, they stopped giving us water for the toilet when they found out we were drinking it. The interrogation and beating continued for over two weeks. After two weeks, things got worse.

From bad to worse:
"I did not even know one of my friends died"

The interrogation continued. I was still blindfolded. Questions were asked from different directions. I thought the questions came from several people because the voices and the tone of them were different for each question.

Then, someone kicked me from the side. I didn't know who it was since I was blindfolded. I went unconscious. When I woke up, I was in my cell and that was when I realised one of my ribs was broken. They also dripped melted-plastic-hot-drips onto my body. They continued the interrogation for days. I also lost one of my teeth from the punching and kicking. There was kicking, beating, punching and they treated us as they wanted. One of us died. A male student. He died at the interrogation centre.

No one knew. I did not even know one of my friends died from the interrogation. We found out the death of our friend at the hospital. They kept us over 40 days at the military interrogation center. Then they sent us to prison. But, prison did not accept us. There were back and forth negotiations between the MI, court and prisons. The court said it will not accept us unless the wounds are healed because we were kids, and MI should not beat kids. So, they took us to the hospital.

No doctors came to treat us. We were put in a room with other prisoners. We were in a bad shape. I, for example, kept throwing up chunks of blood. I was unable to use my hands. But they did not give me any medical treatment until my mother arrived. They did not want to pay for the medical fees for me, for us. My mother paid for me. I was in a bad health condition when my mother arrived, I needed immediate medical attention.

After I got better, they brought us to court and they sentenced us. We were brought to court. We had no say. They read our sentences from a sheet and that was it. [They sent me] to Myeik prison. After one month there, they sent me to Insein prison.

We were sentenced at that court for 14 years. We found out about another 10 years [sentence] at Insein Prison. Total of 24 years. Myeik prison sentenced us for 14 years. We thought that was our sentence. When we arrived in Insein Prison, they asked me, 'What is your sentence?' And I said, '14 years.' But they said, 'No, you are sentenced for 24 years.' I was shocked.

Life in Insein prison:
"For three years I had no one to talk to"

I was imprisoned in Insein prison for four years. I was alone in my cell. The food they [the prison] gave was very bad. There were ants and cockroaches in the food. My parents gave me money to buy food in the prison. And they came to see me in person once a month.

After about two years in Insein prison, I was hospitalised. I did not know what was happening to me. They said that my psychological state was not stable. I had no one to talk with in my cell. See these ants here [points to the ants on the floor]. When I see them, I feel good. They were my friends when I was in prison. I gave food to them and the geckos. I talked to them. I was very lonely and they were my only friends.

Because of this and my unstable mental condition, people and prison guards thought I was very unstable mentally for over a year or two. For three years I had no one to talk to and I was like that.

I had neighbors during the last year. Back then, many activists were arrested. I still was alone in my cell, but there were others in other cells close by. In 1998, there were many arrested. I had people to talk to. The psychological doctors also came to talk to me about my condition and situation.

Mawlamyine prison:
"They gave me [rice] glue to eat. I had no choice"

They moved me to Mawlamyine prison from Insein prison after four years. It was bad in Mawlamyine as well, especially the ex-military soldiers who were now guards or in charge of prison or in charge of interrogation. They were ruthless and inhumane. It has to do with the bad government.

They did not care about anything but money. They did not care about human rights. In prison, the jail owner [the head of prison] allowed to sell everything – from pens and pencils to radios - with double or triple price. A radio in the market cost 3,000 Kyat, but in prison 15,000 Kyat. It was all about money. I bought two radios. My mother paid for them.

I smuggled in some books with the newcomer prisoners around 1998 and 1999 and I got caught. They chained me with heavy iron rods. They punished me like that for two weeks. No food. Instead, they gave me [rice] glue to eat. I had no choice. I ate a few bites, then, stopped for a while, and then took a few bites again. If I hadn't eaten it I would have died.

Free but not free:
"MI, police and the military authorities did not allow people to talk to me"

I was released on September 19th, 2009. My grandmother picked me up in Mawlamyine. [I felt] not at all [free]. The thing is I had been separated from my parents for so long that I was not attached to them.

Prison life was difficult, but also life outside of prison was harder. When I was released, I went to live with my grandmother. Then, I went to Dawei and no one talked to me. There were people who knew me, but they were scared to talk to me.

For example, there was a teashop. I went there every day. People got up and left when I got there. So, I was curious about it and asked the shopkeeper. The shopkeeper said that it was better for me to not to come to his shop, instead, he would deliver the tea to me. I said, 'Why?' And he said that MI, police and the military authorities did not allow people to talk to me.

We [the friends who were sentenced together] were released together. It was the first time I met them again in 15 years. I was happy to see them. But they were imprisoned again. After we all were released, I came here [to Thailand]. They went back inside and continued to do politics and they got arrested and imprisoned again. So, they were imprisoned twice.

Heavy price: "I want people and generations to know what they have done to us"

I don't feel regret. I don't feel hurt. I have done what I think was right, and it is in the past now. And generally, feeling regret or hurt is not good for us anyway.

Only at times when people do not appreciate what I have done or when people don't know what I went through and judge me, I do feel hurt. People [politicians] nowadays just take the pride in what great things they are doing now, but they do not want to mention what others did for them to be here today.

The elders say, I should forgive the military regime. I told them, 'I cannot forgive the military regime.' I am not going to hurt them, but I cannot forgive them. I am not going to pray that they would suffer as I did but I cannot forgive them. I lost everything! First, I lost my education. Second, I lost my social life. Third, I lost my economic well-being. You see. I lost everything.

One thing I want is they should be ashamed of their actions. *Like what's happening today?* Students and monks take to the streets and ask to raise education budget. The military arrested the students and monks. You see. *What do they need to do that for?*

I will not harm them, but I want people and generations to know what they have done to us and what they are capable of doing. You see, in our family, my parents and my two brothers and one sister finished universities. But, I did not. I did not finish my education, and I was imprisoned, and this happened to me.

I am very mad at the government group. I will not forget

them. I am going to bring them to court some day for justice. They arrest people and charge people unfairly. I am going to put charges on them for their actions toward me when the next government is elected - a democratic government.

x   x   x

Soe Lwin came to Thailand in 2009 after he had again been taken to the police station for talking about how the government should repair the road outside his house.

He arrived in Umpiem refugee camp, but felt discriminated against as he was not of Karen ethnicity and could not speak the Karen language.

He now lives in the Thai border town of Mae Sot where he earns a living working in a restaurant, and studies English during his free time.

He is still on regular medication and has to have an x-ray on his ribs and chest every four months due to the injuries sustained during his interrogation back in 1994.

Thazun

" If Men Can Do These Things, I CAN also Do These Things "

Young Arakanese Woman *Thazun*

Thazun is a courageous, beautiful and talented young Arakanese [Rakhine] woman who talks openly about her life and experiences. Despite being forced to spend her childhood separated from her politically active father, and being almost starved to death as a result of forced labour demands imposed on her mother, Thazun has never given up hope. Her determination for a better life has led Thazun to make brave choices that have given her a chance to study in one of the most prestigious schools on the Thailand-

Burma border. Along the way, Thazun has had to challenge her world view and learn that women should be treated as equal members of the society, despite loud objections from not only men and elderly people in her community but sometimes women themselves. Thazun now knows that nothing is impossible when you put your mind and heart to it.

"As I was young
I didn't really know about hunger or that
I should eat two meals per day"

When Thazun was about five years old, she was facing near starvation as a result of forced labour demands imposed on her mother. Thazun's mother was among hundreds of others who were forced to work on a government bridge building project in Rambree Township, Arakan State. People from over 30 villages were forced to leave their families in order to search and collect stones for the bridge. Meanwhile, Thazun's father was involved in politics and had no choice but to stay away from his family.

My mother had to work for forced labour in the road construction… it's like connecting two islands with a road. They had to collect big stones and take them there. From each village 10 or 20 families had to work for the project.

My mother and father weren't with us, and we had no friends' parents to look after us. And my sister was the eldest in the family so she had to collect food and look after us. She was very young too, only 15 or 16 years old. Sometimes we had nothing to eat. Sometimes we ate only one meal per day. Just only rice with some salt. My mother lived away for more than two years. She was able to come back once or twice a month, because when there is high tide, you can't collect sand and stones in the island.

My mother appealed to the authorities and they gave her one time, maybe after 10 months, and she came back. She was very upset because we were almost dying.

Yeah, my mother was very skinny [when she came back]... and maybe because she worked too hard, and her eyes were very... She said later it made her feel very sorry. I don't know how to express that word because it's something deep inside your heart. When you see your children dying of hunger and... No one really cared for them.

Then Thazun's mother had to go back and leave her children again, this time for one year and 2 or 3 months.

I can't remember exactly. She didn't actually get a break, she fled. She couldn't bear living there. All the waters were salty, the rivers, everything was salty. My mother said you couldn't wear your shirt for more than two or three days because it tears from the salt.

And you couldn't get fresh water, there was no water, everything was salty. You could barely get drinking water, you also had to wash yourself in the salty water. So everyone was suffering from some diseases and some people died there.

My mother was afraid that if she died, all her four children would be left alone. When I was young I didn't know all those things, but later she told me.

"Sometimes they came in the middle of the night to our house with guns, looking for my father"

When Thazun was still very young, authorities would come to their house and ask about her father. Sometimes they would interrogate her mother.

It was really a bad time. When they came to look for my father in the house they would sometimes take my mother to an interrogation center. You have to go there if you are charged with anything and explain. They ask lots of questions. My mother said she had to go there 5 or 6 times. Sometimes they came in the middle of the night to our house with guns, looking for my father. My mother was very afraid. At the time one of our grandmother was staying with us and she cried a lot.

My father fled to Bangladesh. He had to flee because there

were posters on the walls searching for my father. He was one of the leading figures in the 88 democracy uprising. So he no longer could stay in the township or in our home country... he had to flee to Bangladesh. During the 88 uprising I was only about 3 or 4 months old.

After Thazun's father went to Bangladesh the family moved away from Sittwe where Thazun was born. In 1999 Thazun got a chance to go to Bangladesh and meet her father.

For 10 years maybe I didn't see my father. Since I was young I didn't know my father. I was very surprised because before I met him I dreamt of him... When I went there one of my grandmas, said; 'Listen your father is coming!' And I recognised him because I already saw him in my dream. He was wearing one of these patterned shirts and even in my dream he was wearing the same shirt. I had the dream maybe two times. It was something like magic, because I had never seen my father and we don't have photographs.

"When I learnt about that [women's rights] I could see that we have been abused for a long time"

*After finishing school, Thazun joined Rakhine Women's Union (RWU) in Bangladesh. Thazun explains that the organisation **has** good relations with Women's League of Burma as well as other local* *organisations. For the first time ever, Thazun was faced with women's issues and started to open her eyes to a new reality.*

In the organisation we didn't have that many educated girls, and women's rights is something we didn't really know about. So the chairperson introduced us the principals of human rights and she taught us everything.

I got lots of skills there, for the first time I learnt about women's rights. And when I learnt about that I could see that we have been abused for a long time… They have that hierarchy in their mind and they think they are superior to women. On the other hand, it's very hard to break down their rules, because they've been used to it. It's very very hard.

They think that women can't make good plans or work for development or for the future. So for education, they think that if you educate 12 girls it's equal to educating one boy. If you educate one boy he can lead others, but if you educate 12 girls none of them might be able to do that.

A good housewife is quite opposite to what is believed in with women's rights. They are good at cleaning the house and looking after the children. They should be good to the husband's family. Should be educated and lead her husband to be good. If he is still a bad guy after marrying the girl, then she is not a good housewife. A good housewife should lead the husband to be a good man. If he is not, it's the woman's fault. Everything depends on the wife. She also has to cook delicious meals.

"If we want to fight for women's rights, we have to fight a lot"

I think we still need lots of lobbying and campaigning about women's rights. The first thing is for women to know their rights. If they know their rights, they can protect themselves. But still it's quite hard to persuade them. They are afraid of their families and elderly people who think that these things are bad and against the religion.

I think Burmese government is not very different from our community men. They don't give priority for women. That's why our democracy leader like Aung San Suu Kyi faces a lot of trouble, because she is the only woman. Some people say she is only in this position because of her father, but it is also something about her. She got this position because of her abilities and capabilities, but some people don't really believe that. If we want to fight for women's rights, we have to fight a lot.

I want girls to have equal rights with men. I believe that if men can do these things, I can also do these things because I have my education and I have my skills just like any man. When I first heard about women's rights, I thought it was weird. Going against older people and the law. It was very strange for me at first, but later I found out that we really need these things, because we have been abused for a long time, and we didn't really know we had been abused.

When Thazun was working for RWU she got a chance to attend an internship in Bangkok with ALTSEAN-Burma, and so had to travel from Bangladesh to Mae Sot. Thazun and her friend traveled across the country, stopping to be investigated at a number of gates, sometimes bribing the authorities and other times being allowed to continue for free. They traveled across rivers and on windy mountains roads on motorbikes, line cars, boats and busses, spending nights in guest houses and homes. After finishing the internship, she made the same journey back to Bangladesh and worked for the RWU.

"The education system is very bad, and very poor"

As her parents were getting older, Thazun started feeling that she should do more to support her family. Thazun traveled across the country again and started working at a market in Mae Sot sewing clothes.

I knew how to sew clothes. I didn't get proper wages, sometimes only 40 baht for a day. Then I just decided that I should work in a factory. I started to work in a factory for three days, but I couldn't really work there. I don't know how other people manage to work in a factory. I just couldn't do it.

And then one day one of my brothers [friend], who is a student in ACU (Australian Catholic University), told me that there is an ACU program where you can study for diplomas. And I thought I should get education first to have a better job, and to support my family. When you are skillful and have greater knowledge, you can also do greater things for your country and for the community.

So I just applied for ACU and… Luckily I was chosen for ACU. I think from education we can have some changes. Many of the civilians are not educated, and they can't really have self-confidence. They are under the control of the government. And when they are not educated they don't really know how to overcome obstacles.

The education system is very bad, and very poor. Sometimes students cheat in the exams, but the teachers just pass them. They give them money and the teachers pass them… It's quite disappointing and it's a very sad story for the Burmese people. We don't know where we stand and we don't have a good future.

When I was studying there [in Burma] we were speaking in Arakanese, but later everyone had to speak Burmese. They took Burman teachers and put them in our schools. It was very hard for the people because most of them couldn't understand Burmese, they couldn't understand the teachers or the lessons. They still have Burman teachers there. They don't know Arakanese; they just speak Burmese.

"Because you are doing something right you are being put into prison"

My father always supports me for education. My father has worked for politics his whole life. His dream is that he wants one of his children to follow his path. So most of the children are now with their families and if they can't really work for their communities, at least he hopes I can be one of them.

I honestly have quite strong feelings for politics. I want to do something for the community and for my organisation, and maybe for Burma one day. After I finish, I'm going to further my education, I want to have a good scholarship if I get a chance.

I have heard from some of my friends that you can talk about politics openly now but you can't really turn your words into action. If you are organising a movement or something, then you will be cut.

When you are being abused, you have to go against it. And it's very clear that when you are going against it and doing something right, because you are doing something right you are being put into prison. It's quite hard to understand the government's role. They say that you can do politics freely and you can lobby the people if you are doing good for the country. In the meantime they are arresting the youth and they are putting them into prison.

x   x   x

Since graduating from the ACU, Thazun has been working to advance women's participation in decision making and advocating for women's rights in her native Arakan State.

Thazun aims to go to university to study political science in order to one day help her people and work for her country through participating in politics, just like her father.

" FREEDOM is
More Important than Anything "

Karen Major General *Nerdah Bo Mya*

Nerdah Bo Mya was born in a small Karen village in a KNU (Karen National Union) controlled area near Manerplaw—the former headquarters of the KNU and the pro–democracy movement—as the son of the late General Bo Mya who was the President of the KNU from 1976 to 2000. After being educated in Thailand and in the USA, the young graduate's short visit to the Thailand-Burma border turned into a life-long mission, as Nerdah witnessed the 1994 Karen split from the KNU in what he describes as 'the blackest day' of their history. Nerdah realised that he had to stay and do something for his people who otherwise 'will not survive.' He started working for KNU foreign affairs, meeting with diplomats and politicians, spreading international awareness about the Karen struggle for freedom and equality. A few years later he became a battalion commander and fought in the front lines against the Burmese army, painfully witnessing many of this comrades killed and wounded in the battle fields. After two decades of indescribable hardship and unwavering dedication for the cause, Nerdah is now the Major General and the Chief of Staff of the Karen National Defence Organisation (KNDO). This empathetic "rebel" leader emphasises that it is not just the Karen people but the whole nation of 60 million people who are still suffering and need to be freed.

Manerplaw:
"My father set up the headquarters for the Karen people"

I remember when I was a child. I grew up near the border area, close to Manerplaw, the old [KNU] headquarters. I grew up in Htoo Wah Lu village, a very small village. We had only few houses near by our house and we played together with some of the kids that we were growing up with. We were staying together like one big family, even though we had different houses.

We grew up in a KNU controlled area. My father set up a small school for us, like primary school. The school had Karen curriculum, all mostly Karen curriculum. Then later on, my father, because the community was enlarging, he set up a high school. We called it Karen State high school. We didn't really actually know about the political problems or the fighting, because the community where we were brought up was very peaceful and our neighbors were mostly Karen people.

Then I heard about the fighting, the political problems, and then the refugees started moving into Thailand. And then I realised that Karen people are not recognised and we need to gain back our freedom. They started talking about these things and every Friday the KNU leaders would come to our school and talk about the political situation, the military situation, and the refugees. So we listened and we learned, and I realised then, 'we've got a problem.'

When I was about to finish high school, there was big fighting and then my father set up the headquarters for the Karen people. It was called Manerplaw at that time. He was looking for the place and then he took my hand and showed me around, and he said he is 'going to set up the headquarters for the Karen people.' So he set up the headquarters, and he moved back and forth from the village to the headquarters.

Soldiers lined up in Manerplaw in 1994. (Photo: Thierry Grandidier)

Education:
"I always had in my mind that one day when I graduate I will come back and help my people"

When I was about to finish high school my father arranged something for me, to go to Bangkok to study. I stayed there until I was 22 and finished high school. Then some teachers tried to convince me to continue my education, and they talked about the Pacific Union College [in California] that was connected to my school in Bangkok. So, in 1989, I took my first travel to America and I started college.

I had a cultural shock [in the US], because the culture was so different, in the beginning. But I adapted, I tried to adapt to the new society and new culture. Because I had to be on my own, I had to be more flexible, and try to adapt to how to live with friends, how to live with other people, even though I felt different. There were some Karen people, but the school where I went, it was only me. I was the only Karen.

I stayed there altogether five years to finish my Bachelor's degree in America. Even though I studied abroad, I read about the refugees, the Karen refugees coming across the border [from Burma to Thailand], and the oppression of the Karen people by the Burmese, and I always had in my mind that one day when I graduate I will come back and help my people.

Coming back:
"Some of our territories had been taken by the Burmese army"

In 1994 I came back. I came back and after one week the DKBA (Democratic Karen Buddhist Army – now known as Democratic Karen Benevolent Army) split from the KNU, and then the problem started. I wanted to go back [to the US] and continue my education, but when I came back, one week later the DKBA split, and then I realised 'now I have to do something for my country. Otherwise my people will not survive.'

Since then, I started to work for my people and try to help my father and the KNU. When I first joined the KNU, they asked me to be part of foreign affairs. I got to meet with a lot of people, in Bangkok, and talk with diplomats all over the world and also with military attaché. And also I tried to raise awareness of the current situation and the political situation, and talk to them and explain to them more clearly about what we are going through and what we should deserve as a nation and as a Karen people.

I had been working for the KNU foreign affairs for several years when they asked me to be a battalion commander. Then I started working in the field and tried to recruit more people and I recognised that we have to get back our territories. Some of our territories had been taken by the Burmese army. After the DKBA split away from the KNU, they got many of our territories. Deep down inside, I wanted to take it back from our enemies.

Working as a battalion commander:
"Of course you have to give your life - but without freedom we are just a slave"

I have gone through many battles and I am really blessed

that I haven't stepped on a landmine because many of them [soldiers] stepped on landmines, even when we were walking in the battlefield, some people even walked behind me and they stepped on them.

As a commander I always had to think about how to overcome obstacles, and how to retreat. Sometimes I couldn't sleep, because I worried about them [soldiers]. I knew they have their families, maybe some of them might get killed and some of them get wounded. Sometimes it was hard, especially when they got wounded and they died. Their wives came to the basecamp crying and it was really painful. I wanted to help them but I couldn't do anything as a commander. And that's why the hardest part was when I had to do an operation, first of all, I wanted to make sure I do my duty very well, make a good plan, and make a good strategy. So that everybody could be safe as much as possible.

I had to go through these kinds of things, quite often, when I was a battalion commander, when there was fighting. Going through all kinds of hardship, it makes you really sad. But overall freedom is the most important thing for our Karen people, and this is something we have to go through. You can't really avoid it. Of course you have to give your life, you have to give your, some parts of the body, your sweat, your blood. But without freedom we are just a slave, so freedom is more important than anything. I joined the Karen struggle because I want my people to be free. I want democracy.

Nerdah's struggle to help his people: "If you die with honor and you die as a free man it's better than to die as a slave"

In 1994 I started working for the Karen people. The end of 1994 the DKBA problem started. They split away from the KNU and there was, I think, the blackest day of our history. We had to go through a lot of hardship and suffering and all kinds of pressure from all sides, from the Thai side, also from internal conflict and... It was very difficult for us and I thought many times, 'how could we survive?' There was no safe place on the Thai side and also not easy to stay inside, because the Karen were fighting each other. That had never happened in history. That was the first time. So I realised, 'now I really got to do something for my people.'

People deserve freedom, and it really hurts me because I see that our people are very intelligent, very peaceful people, but they have been oppressed and they are not recognised by the government. So we have to try. We have to put ourselves together and try really hard, so that we will be recognised as human beings. This is what I have been telling them, my people, and the soldiers. We want to have freedom.

Freedom is not easy. We have to go through a lot of obstacles, hardship. But if you don't have a clear vision, then sometimes, when you are facing with all kinds of problems, you want to give up. But if you really have a clear vision, for yourself, for your family, for your community, and for your nation, then you will never want to give up. Freedom is more important than anything. If you die with honor and you die as a free man it's better than to die as a slave.

Karen united:
"This is the turning point for Karen victory"

Right now I see our people scattered all over the world. Some of them are in refugee camps, some are scattered along the border here. Some of them are in different countries and they have been resettled abroad. I have realised that we are a big nation, and if we really struggle for our rights and really ask for our rights, our rights cannot be ignored. I keep trying for different factions of Karen armed groups to come back together, so that one day we could be recognised. If we have arms, we should be working for the Karen people, protecting the rights of the Karen people and standing up for the Karen people as a nation.

I was so happy [when the DKBA came back in 2010] and I thought 'this is the turning point.' I thought 'this is the turning point for Karen victory.' Even though we'd been fighting with them for so many years, I felt like we were brothers, fighting each other. I had no blame against them, I just wanted to hug them. I felt so happy.

We were fighting each other for 17 years, before they came back. Right now, they are working together with us and facing the enemy [Burmese military]. So for me, I feel very happy, and I am not afraid of the Burmese army because if our people are not fighting each other my head is clearer than before. I am not afraid, because in the past when we had been fighting with the DKBA, we were facing our people and at the same time the Burmese, the enemy, so it was a really bad time for us. Because if you were fighting with DKBA and then you killed them, the Burmese were clapping their hands. If they killed you, the Burmese were clapping their hands. So, this was something I felt like I wanted to get out of. I really want to fight the Burmese straight on and not fight with my people.

Present and future:
"We need a free democratic government"

When you look at everything on the surface, it seems like everything is now OK. But at the same time the Burmese [military] are taking advantage of the ceasefire situation, and they're moving their troops in and sending supplies, and rebuilding their outposts, in our territories. So what they really want is to occupy our territories, and what we want is to preserve our identity. So we are going opposite ways.

I think with this government, it's not easy to get peace, because their strategy is totally different. Their strategy is to wipe out all the ethnic groups. We cannot trust the government, the government is not sincere for peace talks. The mentality is that they don't change, they just take out their uniforms and inside is still the same thing. The government is playing the game, and trying to manipulate the Karen people. In the old days they used to divide and rule, divide and conquer. They're still using that these days.

All the ethnic groups, they want to preserve their identities, because they have their own history, they want to preserve it. They want to preserve their culture. And it has been forbidden by the government, for many many years. That's why we still have this kind of conflict and fighting, between the Burmese government and the ethnic groups.

And it's not only the ethnic struggle for ethnic rights, we're talking about 60 million people, they're human beings, and they shouldn't be under this kind of government. This brutal government is not really thinking about the people and they're not supporting the people. They shouldn't be running the country. In the future, I think that this government cannot go on for long. One way or

another they have to let it go. But through bloodshed or through peaceful means, we will see. We need a free democratic government, and a country where our people can enjoy equality and human rights.

I've been fighting the Burmese regime for 20 years already, but I fight because I love my people. Not because I hate the Burmese people. I only want to see freedom. If I could exchange my life for freedom I would for my people.

x   x   x

" *FREEDOM is More Important than Anything* "

Karen Major General *Nerdah Bo Mya*

" We Had Never Heard about HUMAN RIGHTS in the Village "

Young Palaung (Ta'ang) Woman *Lway Chee Sangar*

Lway Chee Sangar is 23 years old. The ethnic nationality group to which she belongs, called the Palaung or Ta'ang, has been caught in an armed struggle for self-determination against the brutal Burmese regime for the better part of the past five decades. Lway Chee Sangar began working with the Palaung Women's Organization (PWO) about three years ago when her parents, desperate to give her an opportunity to improve her life, sent her from their tiny, remote village in the northern Shan State to the PWO's former training center in China. It took her a combined six months of training to begin to grasp the idea that all humans have rights. Sangar's story is speckled with brushes with conflict, starting from her birth. She was born on the run, when her parents had to flee their village due to an outbreak of fighting nearby. Still today, the Ta'ang National Liberation Army (TNLA), the armed wing of the Palaung State Liberation Front (PSLF), is fighting off Burmese offensives and combatting opium cultivation in Palaung areas. Civilians are often caught in the cross-fire, and Burmese forces are known to use brutal tactics against civilians in conflict areas, including deadly forced portering and forced labor, torture, killing, and extortion of money, supplies, and drugs. Still, Lway Chee Sangar's main concern was for attaining education.

"I didn't have many rights"

When I was young, I started to go to school, maybe at six or seven years, I don't know. I started to go to school in our village. But when I was young, for our lives, for our food for our family, we did not have a lot of food or a lot of other things... I remember we'd have some rice and we would mix bamboo or pumpkin. Yes, we cooked a lot of soup. We just ate like this when I was young.

I couldn't live with my parents because at that time my parents would have to find work, sometimes they would have to go someplace else and they wouldn't have a place to sleep, they'd sleep in the forest. Sometime, they would just go to another house and work on a tea farm to get money for food for our family. So I just was living with my grandfather. Now, there are only six people in my family including my parents. We are doing better now than we were when I was young.

When I finished my primary school; I started go to Namkhan Township for middle school. I went from my village to Namkhan Township, after maybe two or three days I would arrive there, just walking. At that time we didn't have money to take a taxi or anything, so I just tried walking to go to school. When I arrived at Namkhan I just lived with another family who had come to our village to sell clothes and other things, from Namkham, so I just went and lived with them, in their house.

I didn't have money from my parents. I didn't have a holiday like other people. I just tried to work to get money. Sometimes I tried to go to the forest to get [spices] and vegetables to sell to other people. After two years I went back to our village. I didn't want to go to town because I didn't have money, so I just changed my school to one near our village, they had a big village.

When I finished after two years in that village I had to stop my school for one year to work for my family. I worked as a tea farmer, and sometimes I had to work for other people to get some food to support my family.

"I didn't get any contact with my parents"

In 2008 I stopped my schooling. 2009 I asked my parents, 'I want to go to school again,' and they just tried for me to get money and to send me to go to school. So in 2009 I started to go to school again for my high school (nine and ten standard) in Mogok.

At that time, the same like when I lived in Namkhan, I didn't have money. But I didn't have a chance to get it from outside because we just stayed in a monastery. The monk, our monks, they didn't let us go outside. If we live outside we would have to pay a lot of money, so we just tried to live with monks in the monastery. In the monastery you don't have to pay for food or living, we just had to buy our books and bag.

When I attended my ten standard, I became sick and our teachers who live with us in monastery hospitalised me in January or February 2010. I had to stay 4-5 days in the hospital. After a couple of weeks I started to be better and tried to go to school. But, I couldn't catch up because when I was sick our teachers passed through a lot of subjects. Then, after that didn't recover, I got sick often, I couldn't pass my 10 standard.

After two years I wanted to go see my parents in my village.

I didn't have money to get a taxi or a car to go back. I tried to walk. Mogok to our village is maybe three or four days [walk away]. At the time I walked with other people I didn't know. Because it was very hot we had to sleep in the day and walk at night. Sometimes, two or three am we started to walk. If the sun came we had to stop. Just walking like that and I got to my village, it was 2010.

2010, I couldn't pass my ten standard [exam]. I tried to pass my ten standard but my family was not ok. I tried to ask my parents, 'I want to go to school again, I want to try to pass my ten standard,' but my family was not ok so I just decided, 'I have to stop my school and I have to work for the family'...That is my life when I was young.

"I knew if lived in the village I wouldn't have a chance for anything"

When I stopped my school, I just worked in the village. But sometimes I would think, 'I want to go outside, China, or another place, I want to work, I want to get money,' and sometimes I wanted to make business. I wanted to take tea from one village and sell to another village. But my parents wouldn't give me permission to go like this because they know it is dangerous for a woman, so they didn't give me permission.

I tried to work in the village. At that time, we grew rice and

I had to take care for rice the whole year. When we were done it was maybe six or seven pm. We would take a bath and maybe seven or eight eat dinner, and then I slept. I really wanted to sleep because in the morning I was very tired, so I had to sleep. The next day we would wake up at five am, cook for the family, eat breakfast and maybe six or seven go to work.

In 2011, Lway Chee Sangar wanted to return to school to pass her ten standard exam, but for lack of financial means, was unable. Still, she knew she needed to find a way out. In her village, opportunities for boys are prioritised over those for girls– and most girls marry young.

Some girls marry, as young as thirteen or fourteen years in the village, not only in our village, in our area, a lot of girls, they don't have a chance to go to school. A lot of girls, [get to] maybe five or six standard, some have to stop at three or four standard. Some girls, they don't have a chance when they are young, really. The boys, they have more chances than girls. I know, in my village, a lot of boys can speak in Burmese and they can write and read. But for girls, a lot of girls, they don't know.

Women also don't have access to the same leadership positions. When the heads of village houses congregate to discuss management of the community, only men are allowed to participate. In fact, women can only attend if there are no men still alive in their family. Even then, they are not permitted to speak in the discussion.

In 2011 my brother (friend in the village) who had joined the TSYO (Ta'ang Student and Youth Organisation), I don't know what he and my father talked about, but after they discussed, my parents said to me, 'You have to go with your brother, for your life and for your knowledge, you can improve your skills and everything. If you stay in the village you will get married early and if you get married in the village you will get a drug addict,' because there are a lot of drugs in the village. Men use drugs and drink alcohol every day.

I'm not sure if they knew or not about the PWO. They just told me, 'You should go with your brother.' I asked them, 'Where will I go?' They didn't know. 'If you arrive at the place, you will know.' … I think maybe they did know, but they didn't tell me.

"We had never heard about human rights in the village"

Lway Chee Sangar arrived to China, where she joined the PWO, of which she knew almost nothing about.

I just knew the PWO is an organization… After that we started training first, about human rights. But at that time I didn't know, we had never heard about human rights in the village. Not only me. In our group of people, none of us knew what they were teaching meant. We were just listening.

After three months they sent us to go back to the village. After two months, I lived in the village; they called us again for the second training. In the second training I started to know what human rights are, and I know that all humans, if we are human, we have rights. I started to understand. And women's rights, child's rights, a little, I started to know. After the second training I had to go back again in the village. On August 2012, they called again and sent us to Mae Sot for the internship, which was six months.

The PWO internship afforded Sangar the opportunity to continue learning about her rights, to learn about her Palaung culture and language for the first time, computer skills, and English. From here, she was able to earn a spot in the Political Empowerment Program (PEP), based in Chiang Mai, Thailand.

"I have to try to know about politics, to improve my life"

I started to be interested [in politics] when we joined the internship. At that time we could use the internet, the computer. I started to read the news and other things on the internet, on websites. At that time I started to learn about the situation in Burma. I knew I also have rights. Because if we are humans, when we are born we have rights. But I never knew about this. I have to try to know about politics, to improve my life.

At that time I knew the situation in my village and outside my village, in the township, and other women, I knew it was very difficult. So I thought, 'I have lost my rights and my life, a lot, when I was young, until now. I didn't know anything.' I had to try and I had to know what happened in our village and in other places.

I know we have, if we are children, we have child's rights, and we have women's rights. But I never got those rights. Because when I was young I just faced a lot of work, and work for family, trying to go to school. Now I know, if we are children we can go to

PWO training in Northern Shan State. (Photo: PWO)

school, the government has to provide free school for basics, for primary school, they have to open for the children. I know that. But for us, we didn't get that chance when we were young. We had to try to get money to go to school. And for education we have to try everything, so I knew I lost my life. Now, some children get the chance to go to school. A lot of women, now, it's more balanced. We don't have the same discrimination between sex and gender.

Sometimes I also started to tell them in the village we should not have discrimination. Why is it [that] boys have to go to school while girls have to work in the village? Because, as you know … we have to improve our situation. Boys are human and girls are also human.

I want to go back to my village and I want to call people who will understand me and who will take responsibility for the village. I know that if we work for our nation and for our people, we can work for our lives, for the whole life, but I must try to work for my nation and people because I love my nation and people.

x   x   x

Today Lway Chee Sangar is a staff member at the PWO, and she sends the little money she earns doing this to her younger brother and sister. She hopes they will be able to study and pass their tenth standard exams, unlike her.

To this day, armed conflict continues in Palaung lands, and The Palaung State Liberation Front (PSLF) / Ta'ang National Liberation Army (TNLA) is one of the ethnic armed organisations that the Burma Government excluded from the "nationwide" ceasefire agreement (NCA).

Despite the conflict, Sangar has returned to her village three times to see her family and conduct workshops on health, family planning, and the importance of good leadership.

" Our Staff Had Never Experienced How to Do Amputation "

Jungle Medic and Ethnic Health Director *Saw Win Kyaw*

Saw Win Kyaw is a 42-year-old Buddhist Karen man who was born and grew up in Hpa-an Township. Taking to the streets in the 8888 uprising, 17-year-old Saw Win Kyaw and thousands of other students were forced to flee to the jungle after the military took over power. Saw Win Kyaw trained as a medic and in 1995, helped to establish a bamboo hut clinic in the war-torn jungles of northern Karen State. He ran the clinic for over a decade, delivering babies in emergency conditions with no experience, amputating more than 150 limbs with extremely limited equipment, and training hundreds of others in an attempt to promote a community-based health system in an area where health services were completely destroyed. From Burmese army attacks to the threat of landmines and malaria, for Saw Win Kyaw and other jungle medics, these are nothing but 'normal conditions'. In 1998, Saw Win Kyaw joined the Back Pack team and soon after became the field-in-charge for Papun area. He is now the director of the organisation and manages over 300 health workers across rural ethnic areas in Burma. This story depicts his life and experiences in the jungle and beyond.

Growing up in Hpa-an:
"Most people were very angry at the government"

I was born in Hpa-an, the capital of Karen State. I lived there until I was 17 years old. At the time in Hpa-an, they took tax for porter fees. When the Burmese military troops are going to the front lines, porters carry military materials for them. So they arrested a lot of porters: In the cinemas, in the harbour, sometimes they arrested porters in the house. So at night time most men fled to the jungle and they were sleeping and living in the jungle.

At the time they [Burmese military] were fighting in Dawna

mountain areas with the KNU (Karen National Union). That's why we, meaning not only my family but most of Hpa-an people had a lot of difficulties. It was difficult to purchase food and people were also afraid to be arrested for portering. So, most people were very angry in that situation. The government also deleted out the money [the government announced that the three biggest denomination notes were to be replaced and suddenly had no value]. Most people were very angry at the government.

8888 Uprising:
"The whole country, especially students, left to the jungle"

At the time I was 17 years old. I attended school in Hpa-an, I was a high school student in 9th standard. And then in 1988 the student uprising swept through all of Burma. We heard about what happened in Yangon. There was a technological engineering student and a student demonstration in Yangon Institute of Technology. And they broke it down with guns.

I also took part in the uprising and the demonstration. My parents were also very angry and joined the demonstration. We went to the streets in Hpa-an. There were a lot of people. Even most people living in rural areas came to Hpa-an and they demonstrated a lot. Then Ne Win and the government… The military took power.

They announced everywhere in our Hpa-an that the people who are in demonstration sites have to move to other places. If not they will shoot. Most people left Hpa-an. Many many students and many many villagers and civilians moved to the jungle. The whole country, especially students, left to the jungle, the Karen revolution area, the KNU controlled area. I also left.

From Manerplaw to Papun:
"The health program and health activity are totally dead, destroyed"

After the military government took over power, I fled to the jungle and then I arrived in Manerplaw. In 1989 I attended basic medical training in a KNU hospital in Manerplaw for six months. Then from 1992 to 1996 I attended war casualty management training course, a three-year training course. Trainers from Norway, two doctors, they trained us mainly in how to take care of injured patients.

In 1994, Manerplaw fell down. It was 1994 December and 1995 January. At the time DKBA (Democratic Karen Buddhist Army - now known us Democratic Benevolent Army) and KNU were divided and fighting. The military government helped DKBA, and KNU's headquarters Manerplaw fell down. At the time I was working in the Manerplaw base hospital. Most people fled and I also fled to Mae Rah Moe refugee camp together with refugees. I lived there for one or two months because I had to take care of patients in the camp with some medical leaders. One or two months after AMI (Aide Médicale Internationale) arrived there and they set up their hospital and clinic.

Then one of my colleagues said: 'The AMI also is here now and provides a health program. So there is no need for special health care here. We should help our area, we should help them. Because currently the health program and health activity are totally dead, destroyed. If you arrive there you can help.'

Setting up a jungle clinic:
"If we had some medicine then we gave medicine"

After Manerplaw fell to the military government I moved to Papun area. At the time there was a big government military offensive and health and education sector in that area was totally destroyed. That's why I tried to set up one small clinic in the northern Papun area, we call it Dae Bu Noh clinic.

I arrived to Papun on May 15 in 1995. At the time I had nothing. I discussed with some health workers, my colleagues, with

Setting up new clinic in Dae Boe Noh. (Photo: Saw Win Kyaw)

some medics. We discussed that we should set up a small clinic here. But only a bamboo clinic. So we tried to do as much as we can and we set up [the clinic]… We tried to help and take care of the health of the community as much as we could.

But I had only attended basic medical training and how to take care of injured patients. So I faced a lot of problems with other diseases like complicated malaria. Also the delivery cases and taking care of pregnant women were very difficult. At the time I had very little knowledge in how to take care of pregnant women.

The first delivery:
"I did CPR for more than 45 minutes"

There is one experience I had in that area. It was my first delivery case.

One villager called me and he said that 'my wife is pregnant and started having contractions and abdominal pain.' He called me and he said that 'please try to do delivery for my wife.' I replied that it is not my expertise, I can't do it. He said that 'in this area you are the higher level of health department. So at least you can help with something.' I was so scared and afraid at the time, because I can't do it.

This delivery was prolonged labour, meaning it took a very long time. And people suggested that I should abort the baby to save the mother's life. I was so scared and I discussed with the woman, the mother. She said that I'm getting old. I want children, a baby. That's why I don't want to abort my child. If the child dies I will die together with the child, she said. At the time she was 32 or 34 years old, and I was 24 years old. So I compromised with her.

Eventually I found contraction medicine in that area and luckily within three or four hours, there were some more contractions. Somebody was also pushing a little bit, and that baby... we could see the head. But the mother was unconscious. Then... I looked and that baby was coming out but he was very silent. So I cut the umbilical cord and for the mother I had already given some medicine. Then I did CPR for more than 45 minutes. Luckily that baby, that child was also alive. He is very lucky. And the mother... In the next two or three hours, she woke up. Until this day, they are alive. Very lucky.

That was my first experience and I was so scared and afraid.

After that I faced a lot of delivery cases in that area. That's why I came to Mae Tao Clinic and I asked Dr. Cynthia Maung: 'Dr. Cynthia, *thramu* [Karen word for 'teacher'], you should teach us how to do delivery, how to take care of the pregnancy delivery case?' She trained us for one month. We were very lucky. Later when I was faced with those cases I could manage.

Burning the clinic: "I want one thing; a bone saw!"

In 1997, the military government burned down our clinic. Not only my clinic, they burnt the whole village and also the Toe They Del clinic, which is supported by Dr. Cynthia Maung.

We knew they [Burmese military] were coming. We fled together with six landmine injury patients. We had to carry them. It took one week, we lived in the jungle for a week. And we tried to set up the clinic again.

Some material we could bring with us but some material we lost. That's why at the time I asked one of my health leaders: 'I have lost my bone saw, can you help me?' He had just arrived in Bangkok and he met with one Australian doctor, Dr. Kate, an advisory for Mae Tao Clinic. We met Dr. Kate during the Christmas month and she asked: 'Do you want any present for Christmas?' I say 'yes I want one thing; a bone saw!' She sent two bone saws for us.

Landmine injuries:
"Our staff had never experienced how to do amputation"

Especially in 1997 and 1998 until 2000 there was a big offensive in our area and a lot of patients. I did around 150 amputations in Papun area.

The first time, I saw a patient with landmine injury and I brought him back to my clinic. At the time I was not experienced doing amputation for a human. So I wanted to refer him to a Thai clinic or Thai hospital. At the time there was a lot of fighting and the local authority, local commander, he did not allow to send the patient to Thailand. So I decided... It was very difficult for me, but I decided I need to do amputation in my clinic.

At the time we had no blood bags, blood transfusion bags and also our staff had never experienced how to do amputation. I knew because I attended the war casualty management training course. Currently he is still alive.

In my hands one injured patient, landmine patient, died. Because at the time I had not enough blood bags. Most landmine injury patients are dead before they arrive at the clinic. If they arrive at the clinic we can save them. It's not so difficult. We use some surgical material and a saw. It takes about 1 hour or 1.5 hours [to complete the amputation]. We had to use only limited, very limited, amount of materials. Sometimes the thread was not enough and sometimes blood bags not enough, and also sometimes the antibiotic medicine and infusion drip were not enough. But, we had to manage.

Jungle challenges:
"if the military government arrive in our area they will try to burn down our clinic"

When we were working in Papun, we were volunteers. We had nothing, no salary. So we had to ask about food. It was difficult. Now we can communicate directly with some NGOs/INGOs and yes they provide us with medicine, medical material, and some food. But it is very difficult, there is not enough for our staff. But most people still try to help their own community and try to keep working in the clinic.

Another thing is medicine. Sometimes we don't have enough medicine for malaria. In our area the main medicine we need is for malaria, diarrhea and dysentery, and antibiotics for pneumonia. And also medicine for injuries. Sometimes we don't have enough.

During fighting time, we also have to listen to information

of where both sides of the military are moving, the non-state actors and the military government, and when they are fighting. And if the military government arrive in our area they will try to burn down our clinic. That also we are so scared and afraid of. So there are a lot of difficulties.

Setting up a community-based health system: "Now we have more than 300 health workers"

I also trained first aid training to the villagers. I trained how to take care of patients with fever and diarrhea. I had one situation with one person who was cutting wood with a big knife. Accidently the knife cut out his leg and he was bleeding a lot. The area is far away from my clinic, five hours by walking. On the way he was bleeding a lot and he was so pale and almost dead when he arrived. But it would have been very easy to stop the bleeding. Just press with something and tie with bandages and he could have walked from that injury place to my clinic. But they don't know how to stop the bleeding, they left him like that and he was bleeding a lot and they had to send him to my clinic by the hammock. That is so bad. I had to give him back two blood bags. That is why I started giving first aid training to the villagers.

In 1997 when the military government burned down our

clinic we had only four or five health workers. Currently at that clinic there are more than 30 health workers. I took responsibility for that clinic from 1995 to 2008 or 2009. In 1996 or 1997, I started the Burma Relief Centre, and also Mae Tao Clinic started sending medicine to our area for mobile trips.

In 1998 they founded the Back Pack Health Worker Team. Dr. Cynthia Maung together with other ethnic health organisations worked together to found it. We started with 32 backpack teams and currently we have 95 backpack teams. And now we have more than 300 health workers.

Back Pack jungle medics transporting a patient. (Photo: BPHWT)

Joggling commitments:
"I know myself, I need to learn"

Currently I take responsibility for the position of Director of Back Pack Health Worker Team. All my experience is from the jungle. I never used a computer. Then I came here [to Mae Sot] and I tried to type in English and Burmese and Karen. That was very difficult for me. That's why I tried to learn English here and I tried to attend a short course in English lecture. Then last year, I applied for ACU (Australian Catholic University).

Some people told me 'you are so stupid.' Some people told me 'you are so crazy.' At the time Maya my professor she said 'if you study in this school you have to take a lot of time so how can you manage your time, because you're travelling a lot?' Yes I am traveling a lot for field trips and I have to attend some meetings, trainings and seminars. 'Don't worry for that because I will compromise with my team,' I told her. Every day I ran from here to ACU study centre. Sometimes I came back at midnight, and sometimes I went there for the whole Saturday and Sunday.

I explained to my colleagues and I am very lucky that my colleagues understood me and I could delegate work to my staff. They were happy to try to do it. I also discussed with my wife. She also understood me. I am very lucky. Currently I have four children. Sometimes my boss, my top leader said 'you're getting old, why do you study and attend school? No need.' But I have nothing to reply to them. I know myself, I need to learn.

Old and new challenges:
"Most donors are moving to Yangon"

In our current working areas in Kachin and Shan States they are still fighting a lot and there are a lot of offensives. Also in Palaung areas. Another problem in the Karen State is land grabbing. So although the guns are not firing they do have a lot of land grabbing. The villagers in our Karen communities are so scared for the situation.

We hope for the best in the future but one thing that can happen is going back to the conflict. I'm so scared for the Kachin and northern Shan State where they are fighting a lot and also because there is a lot of land grabbing. For our organisation I'm not so worried because now we have a lot of experience, we know how to help.

But currently, most donors are moving to Yangon. They should provide not only through Yangon but also cross-border aid. Our working areas are very remote areas and also most of our working areas are ethnic areas. So if the government or any NGO sends help through Yangon, they are very far away and then they also send their own staff there. One big barrier for that is lack of trust and common language. We have experience for more than ten years so we know how to deal with the communities and how to develop health programs in our areas. International donors should provide for the community based health system. Not directly come and provide their own system... The donors should understand that they need to continue to provide cross-border aid and also community based health activity.

X   X   X

ABOUT THE BPHWT

The Back Pack Health Worker Team (BPHWT) is a multi-ethnic community-based organisation that has been providing primary healthcare in the conflict and rural areas of Burma for over 15 years. The teams deliver a wide range of primary healthcare programs to a target population of over 200,000 internally displaced persons (IDPs) and other vulnerable community members who would otherwise have no access to healthcare. The BPHWT encourages and employs a long-term sustainable community-managed approach where health services are requested by communities and the health workers are chosen by, live in, and work for their respective communities. The BPHWT's work is highly organised and they work in close cooperation with a range of other health actors and ethnic organisations based on the border and inside Burma. Encouraged by recent changes and looking into a democratic Federal Union of Burma in the future, the BPHWT is currently discussing with other health CBOs and ethnic health organisations to converge the government healthcare system with the extensive border-based primary healthcare system. Despite these positive developments, progress is slow and the situation in Burma's rural areas remains dire.

" The British Had No Right to Draw the Borderline

IN THE HEART OF NAGA COUNTRY "

Eastern Naga Leader **W. Shapwon**

W. Shapwon is an Eastern Naga leader and Joint Secretary of the Naga National Council who is still miraculously alive after all his colleagues have been wiped out by Indian and Burmese forces as well as Naga socialists. His native Nagaland was once a free land with rich and unique cultural traditions that varied from village to village, each village ruled by their own chieftains. The faith of the

Naga took an ugly turn after the British divided Nagaland without the consent or knowledge of the Naga who refused to acknowledge an arbitrary borderline that ran through villages, fields, and even homes. After the British left, Indian and Burmese forces occupied Naga homeland, following an agreement by their leaders that the Western part of Nagaland was to be ruled by India and Eastern part by Burma. The Nagas never succumbed to the foreign occupation – Naga warriors have now been fighting for freedom and sovereignty for over six decades.

"They called us the free Naga"

Nagas are from a Mongolian racial group, like Kachin, Karen, Karenni, Chin. We have been living as free people, we had no government, we had no king, but chieftains ruled the villages. So in the past, villages were independent villages. We didn't know about Burmese kings, we didn't know about Indian kings, we didn't know any other kings. We were ruled by our chieftains. The British colonial regime reached our land in 1832. They first reached Western part of Nagaland. That's when people started interacting with the British. Eastern Nagaland, they didn't reach until after 1930 maybe. Then they visited some parts of eastern area. But they didn't annex our area. They called us the free Nagas.

Before our people were not organised as a nation. But after the formation of Naga National Council (NNC) [in 1946], all the villages of free Nagas were brought into a nation.

"How can the British give our land to other nations, without our knowledge?"

After Burma and India got their independence, they became free from the orders of colony. Since 1954, they started to colonise our country. That is when the war started. We didn't go to India, but they sent their armed forced to Nagaland and started fighting with the Nagas. So the war started between us. It is dragging on, unsolved, till today.

India and Burma had no right to invade Nagaland. They had no right to colonise Nagaland again. They themselves bitterly fought against the British colonialism. After they break from the British colony, how can they use the same colonialism against the Naga? They have no right to suppress the Naga people. They have no right to deprive the right of Nagas to be a nation. And the British had no right to give our land to India or Burma without our consent, without our knowledge.

It is our land. Before Burma became independent, and

India, we talked to the leaders. We talked to Aung San and Mahatma Gandhi. They agreed that Nagas have every right to be independent. But after they [Burma and India] got independence they became our enemy, to fight against us. We don't want to fight them! We want to be good neighbors with them. We are not their enemy.

If only they did not suppress us and keep us in the dark… The Nagas may have developed. But now, our country is occupied, our lands are not developed, our people are not developed.

"I sleep in Burma, eat in India"

We think that the British had no right to draw the borderline in the heart of Naga country. The British are so far away from our country. How can they come and draw our border without our knowledge? Because of this border, if our home is in India, our fields in Burma, our kettle going around India and Burma. [For example] Lungwa village, is divided into two parts. So Lungwa villagers have become two nations' citizens. The village chieftain says that 'I sleep in Burma, eat in India.' Because the border crosses in the middle of his house. How can we recognise that as a border?

For more than 60 years now we have been suffering. Many many human rights violations are there! But no organisations are there to report it. Raping, beating, illegally collecting money,

Naga woman grinding rice in a village.
Children in eastern Nagaland (Photos: NNC)

threatening the people and taking their money or their domestic
animals, cows, and pigs. All these things demanded by the Burmese
army officers.

"That day there was heavy rainfall, so they [enemy] couldn't see my footprints"

I'm from the Eastern part of Nagaland, Sagaing Division on
the Burmese political map. I was born on December 21, 1949. I
joined the Naga National Council because I love my people, and I
don't want our country to be dominated by other nations. I want to
fight against other nations who come to dominate our people. I
decided already when I was a student that when I get my education

I will give back to my people. That was my decision. I have faced a lot of danger, a lot of problems, and a lot of difficulty. I have been speaking out what is the truth. So those who are doing wrong, they want to eliminate me.

For decades, numerous groups have tried to assassinate Shapwon in this present day head hunt.

In 1977, the Burmese Army carried out heavy operation in my Heimi Region to kill me or capture me alive. They made three operation groups from east, west and north to give me no escape route. They tried to kill me. They even offered the village leaders a handsome reward to nab me and hand over to them. At first in the beginning these villagers also did not know what I'm working for. So obeying this Burmese army, they attempted to capture me.

I told my boys, 'We should be careful tonight. Both of the village leaders are no good now. We have to sleep vigilantly. We should not take off our equipment and our guns should be loaded. And your rucksack should be kept as a pillow without opening it. They think that we are tired and maybe sleeping like dead.'

At night they came to arrest us. I heard a sound crock crock crock crock, boots, like people going around in the resident. The enemy surrounded us so I woke my boys up. I looked in front of the house, where I saw two men squatted down. I thought they were Burmese Army soldiers and opened fired upon them, and jumped out from the house and took a position to fire more at them before I retreat. But then, unexpectedly, a village leader shouted 'villagers, villagers!' After that I told the boys 'let's go!'

We took some rice and we ran away from that village. It took about one hour from that village to Haman village. We prepared food and again left the village before dawn. That day there was heavy rainfall, so they [enemy] couldn't see my footprints. So I could escape from them. But then when I approached another village, they told me: 'Hi! My younger brother, how did you reach here again? The Burmese army is here, in the field! Go away at once, just now! You cannot sleep in the village.' So I ran away to the jungle again, at night.

"I am one of the top people in their lists to be killed"

In 1978, Muivah, the General Secretary of Naga National Council at the time, wanted to form a socialist government. And he wanted to overthrow the leadership of Phizo. He had formed a new government on the pattern of socialism in August 1976, but most of the Naga army officers did not support him. So from there, they were divided into two; those who supported Muivah's policy and those who did not support it. Muivah and Isak convinced some

Naga army officers to join them, in the last part of 1979, they started killing all those who did not support socialism.

At that time I was lucky because I was sent to go to Kohima in Western Nagaland to meet with veteran Naga national leaders. On my way Indian police arrested me. I was in the lockup when my friends were killed by Muivah and Isak in Eastern Nagaland. In the last part of 1979, Isak and Muivah eliminated all NNC leaders, 18 in total, who refused to support their socialist political ideology. After the elimination of their opponents, they formed the so-called National Socialist Council of Nagaland (NSCN) on January 31, 1980. Since then they have been killing their own people, anyone who refuses to support them. I am one of the top people in their lists to be killed, because I am strongly against their dictatorship and socialism.

I was in jail for two years and more than seven months. I was badly tortured by the Indian police. I was released in March 1982. And then I returned to Eastern Nagaland to serve my nation again. Since then Isak and Muivah's people have attempted to kill me many times.

Shapwon escaped many close calls in the years that followed, including a vicious bear attack.

Bear attacked me in 1995 August. When I came to that place, in defence of his food, it comes and attacks me. The skin on my face falls down, all this face falls down. It took three hours to

Naga Army was formed in the 1950s when the Indian Army started undeclared war with the Nagas. (Photo: NNC)

reach the village. I had stitching materials, and my wife told the villagers to stitch my wound. But the wound was so big, no one dared to touch my wound. I told the villagers: 'You carry me up to the hospital.' Four days they carried me up to the hospital, and we slept in the jungle. Slowly they carried me and finally we reached the Noklak hospital. I was there for more than two months.

After that Shapwon spent five months in Kohima Naga Hospital where the doctors reconstructed his face with the help of donations collected from a Christian aid group in Australia.

"One Day the World Will Recognise Our Sovereignty"

The Naga national policy of Naga National Council is to solve the problems through peaceful means. That is our stand. We want a peaceful solution so we established the Kohima peace camp in Nagaland. In July 1997, an NSCN-IM man attempted to shoot at me from outside the Kohima peace camp. But then, an old man saw the sniper standing behind a tree. He shouted to give a report to the camp guards, and then the sniper ran away. In 1999 also, about 30 Burmese Army soldiers came to my wife's village in order to kill me. But I was not in the village.

Such dangerous things are still there. Many of our leaders, those who stayed in Eastern Nagaland in those days 1976-1979 were killed… I alone remain alive. And I know what happens in Eastern Nagaland, so I can tell all these things. If I am telling all these truths and writing all these things then the people come to know that they [NSCN leaders] are wrong, they have done wrong. Because of that they want to kill me.

I decided to leave Nagaland. It was March 2009. I came to Thailand because I could not stay in our land anymore because of our own people, because of Indian army and Burmese army, all trying to kill me. So, to save my life, I came to Thailand. I think I am alive only because I came to Thailand. If I couldn't reach here I may have been killed, long before.

We should speak the truth. But many people are afraid of speaking the truth because of bullets. Because of bullets in Nagaland. Those who speak the truth are killed. They are after my life not because of I am a liar, murderer or a traitor but because I am telling and stating the truth and do not support their socialism. I am telling the truth because I cannot tolerate false accusations and killings, telling lies and destroying our society.

The NSCN men are committing human right violations in Nagaland but the world does not know it. No one dares to give such human rights violation reports to the outside world. I have written about their terrorist activities and human rights violations. Because of it, I became in their top list to be assassinated. Those who are afraid to speak the truth and keep silent have no danger for their lives.

If the situation changes, then I will have to go back and work for my people. We have to mobilise our people and work together through peaceful means. One day the world will recognise our sovereignty. And the Indian and Burmese people will also recognise our sovereignty and they will unconditionally withdraw their armed forces from our Nagaland. We will have a good relationship with them. That I hope.

If I can work for my people then it is my pleasure. That's all. I don't deserve or want big leadership. But what I can do for my people, I will do.

Our land is not part of India or Burma. India and Burma came to our country. They came to invade our country, they came to colonise our country. The killing among the Nagas started because of the enemy policy. That is one of the enemy policies, to make us kill each other. It's the same in Karen State, Kachin, Shan also, it is because of enemy's policy.

x   x   x

About Naga history

The origin of Naga freedom struggle is traced back to the founding of the Naga Club, in Kohima in 1918 by a group of educated Nagas. They submitted a memorandum to the British to exclude the Nagas from any constitutional framework of India.

With the coming of Angami Zapu Phizo, popularly known as Phizo, the Naga Movement gained momentum in the late 1940s. In 1946, the Naga Club became the Naga National Council (NNC).

The NNC under Phizo's leadership declared
Independence of Nagaland on the 14th of August
1947. Phizo was arrested in 1948 by the Indian
Government on charges of rebellion. On his release,
Phizo was made the President of the NNC in 1950.

The National Socialist Council of Nagaland
(NSCN) was formed on January 31, 1980 by Isak
Chishi Swu, Thuingaleng Muivah and S.S.
Khaplang opposing Phizo's leadership and NNC.
According to them, the Shillong Accord was a
surrendered accord to India, although the
document clearly seems to have been invalid from
the start.

On April 30, 1988, the NSCN split into two
fractions; the NSCN-K led by S S Khaplang, and
the NSCN-IM, led by Isak Chishi Swu and
Thuingaleng Muivah. The split was due to

Khaplang rejecting Isak and Muivah's plan to hold political talks with Indian Government for an autonomous State based on Suisa's proposal. The split triggered a wave of violence and clashes between the factions and different Naga groups.

The violence in Western and Eastern Nagaland continues between different Naga groups as well as between the Naga and Indian and Burmese forces.

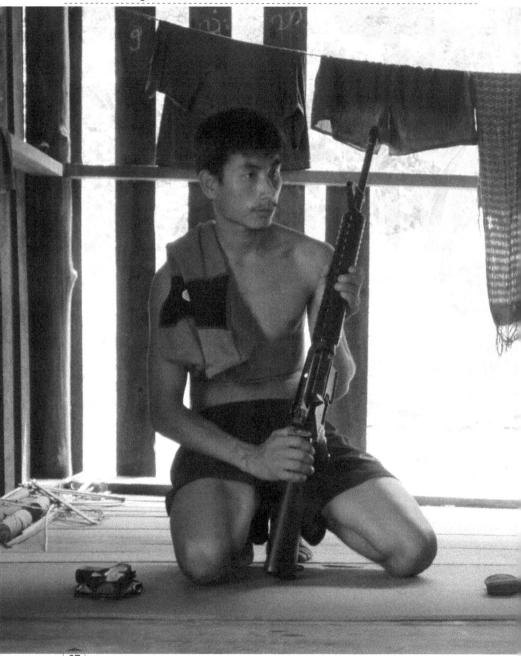

" I Have Never Regretted Becoming a Soldier "

Shan-Karen Freedom Fighter *Shan Lay*

Shan Lay is a friendly, compassionate and dedicated young man from the Shan State who has sacrificed everything to fight for the freedom of his people. Growing up in the Shan State with a Karen mother, young Shan Lay was always interested in learning more about his Karen roots. But his mother didn't speak the language and all he was taught at school was that 'Karen were rebels.' Somewhere deep inside, Shan Lay felt that there was more to the story. He witnessed firsthand the brutality of the government forces: Two of Shan Lay's family members perished in the 8888 uprising, and when Shan Lay was a teenager, the Burmese military confiscated their family farm. Among other villagers, Shan Lay and his three childhood friends were forced out of their homes and left with nothing. A few years later, Shan Lay and his friends became freedom fighters on the Thailand-Burma border. Today, Shan Lay is the only one of them still alive. Despite the heartache, Shan Lay vows to never give up. Not until the country is free.

"When I was at school I was told that Karen were rebels... I wanted to see and know about the Karen, who are the Karen?"

After losing his big sister and grandfather in the 8888 uprising, Shan Lay now has 6 siblings still alive. His father is ethnic Shan and a soldier for the Shan State Army (SSA). Before being perished in Rangoon, Shan Lay's grandfather was also a soldier for SSA. Although Shan Lay's mother is ethnic Karen, young Shan Lay didn't know much about the Karen culture or history.

When I was at school I was told that Karen were rebels. That's all I knew. My mom didn't speak Karen. I wanted to see and know about the Karen, who are the Karen? I didn't like that I was taught that Karen are rebels. I really hated the Burmese for teaching that.

Shan Lay's family made a living growing pineapples and tealeaves in a rural village near Taunggyi, Shan State. When Shan Lay was 14 years old the Burmese military came and confiscated their land and their home to make a training ground for the military. Their plantations were destroyed.

We were given nothing and we lost everything we had. If you refuse to give away your land they will come with a bulldozer and destroy the farm. We had to leave and live with my aunt and uncle in Taunggyi. It was very difficult to manage and to try to find another farm as we had no money or anything.

"I wanted to educate myself more but I knew it was impossible"

I wanted to educate myself more [after finishing ten standard] but I knew it was impossible. My parents couldn't pay for it. Especially after they lost their farm and everything there was no way my parents could have paid for me or my siblings to go to school. They were struggling just to survive.

In his village, Shan Lay had three close friends all of whom were ethnic Shan. Shan Lay and his friends were forced to separate

when the Burmese military confiscated their land.

We stayed in contact. Later we decided to travel to Thailand. We were all from the same village, we left together, and we came to Thailand together. I was 15 years old at the time.

We sneaked in the country and had to pay for someone to take us the Chiang Mai to work. We walked hundreds of kilometers to Chiang Mai, through the jungle. We walked with someone who knew the way. We mainly walked during the night so that we wouldn't be seen by Thai soldiers.

We worked on the border for four years. There were also KNU (Karen National Union) soldiers on the border working to earn some extra money and we made friends with one KNU soldier who worked together with us. At the time I didn't know my friend was a soldier.

"I learned more about the Karen struggle and realised that the Karen were not really rebels"

There was a lot of fighting between the KNU and the Burmese military at the time. While on the border I learned more about the Karen struggle and realised that the Karen were not really rebels. They were trying to make a revolution to set their people free.

In 2004, Shan Lay and his friends joined Karen Revolution Day celebrations in a KNU controlled village and military base camp. At the celebration, Shan Lay saw his friend from the border wearing a soldier's uniform. He was very surprised.

I didn't know he was a soldier until then. I asked his friend if I could also become a soldier. We all joined KNU that day.

Karen Revolution Day is celebrated each year on January 31 to commemorate the beginning of the Karen Revolution.

When Shan Lay became a soldier
he couldn't speak or understand Karen.

I had to use my ears and my eyes and my brains to memorise a lot when I was given training. I had to look at what the other soldiers were doing. I couldn't understand the instructions but I listened carefully and just did what others did. I learned a lot and always did what was asked of me although at first I didn't even understand simple orders like left or right. I tried very hard to learn the language and to be a good soldier.

When asked if he ever thought about becoming a soldier for SSA, Shan Lay says that it's the same being a soldier for the Shan or the Karen army.

We are all fighting for the same cause against the Burmese military.

"I will fight for that until we win
the revolution or I die"

When Shan Lay and his childhood friends joined the army, they were well aware of putting their lives at grave risk. That risk became all too real as soon as Shan Lay began receiving devastating news; one by one, all of his friends perished in the battlefield. Despite the heartache, Shan Lay cannot imagine a life other than that of a soldier.

I train new soldiers, teaching them about landmines and how to shoot and everything that a soldier needs to know. I teach what I have been taught by my commander. I have never regretted becoming a soldier.

I am very good at shooting, and I was always a good student and a good soldier. Everything I was taught I memorised very carefully and always followed my commander's instructions. If I hadn't, I would already be dead.

I would never [leave the KNU to join Border Guard Force (BGF)]. I am completely devoted to the Karen cause and I will fight for that until we win the revolution or I die. I don't know why they [many KNU soldiers] left and I couldn't understand it. If you decide to become a soldier you shouldn't take that decision lightly. You shouldn't just come and then leave.

Karen people should hold each other's hands tightly, if they do that, then nobody can separate them. All Karen people should love their people, their language, their culture. Some Karen don't even know anything about Karen life and culture, they are Karen but they don't know what it's like to be Karen.

Those Karen who changed sides, should think and ask themselves what have they done for their country? General Bo Mya is dead now but his spirit is still here waiting for the day when the Karen win the revolution. We Karen have to fight to win it.

A lot of people have died during this struggle, both soldiers and civilians. Their spirits are all also waiting for the revolution to happen. Some Karen don't know about this, they don't know and they just join DKBA or BGF.

"If you just flee and don't fight for your land you will never get it"

Shan Lay says that Karen people, those who live in third countries or in refugee camps, should think about the reasons why they had to flee and why it is that they have to live away from their homeland.

Because of the torture and the difficulties they had in Burma they fled away to refugee camp or to third countries. But if you just flee and don't fight for your land you will never get it. If you want your land and your country then why don't you come back and fight for it.

If you just shout that you want your country nobody will come and give it to you. General Aung San also said that if you want your country then you have to fight for it.

The Karen have been waiting and longing to win the

revolution and to go back for so long. But we still have to fight for it. We haven't won it yet. In the situation now, with the ceasefire between the Burmese military and KNU, the Burmese are calling the Karen soldiers to go back to Karen State. A lot of Karen have been waiting for this for so long that they really want to believe the Burmese.

"They say if we want peace we must give up our weapons. But how can we trust them?"

The Burmese say that you can go back but you need to give up your arms. They say if we want peace we must give up our weapons. But how can we trust them? What if something happens, then we can't do anything.

Long-term peace is different. This is what is needed and it is a big decision to make it. Some people believe them [the Burmese military] too easily and they are easily deceived. The Burmese military can just try to bribe you with money or giving you a car, they can deceive you. You shouldn't believe that. If you give them all your weapons one day they can attack you and kill you when you turn your back... I don't want to kill people but if the Burmese military keeps fighting we have to fight back.

For example, if there is an agreement or friendship between

the Burmese military and the Karen, then the Burmese will say that they will not attack Karen areas. But after that, they will keep coming and learning about our land, give money to people to try to separate the Karen and make them fight each other.

The Burmese say now things have changed and there is a ceasefire. So they should pull their troops away. But they haven't moved their troops. They have actually been sending more and more food and weapons for the soldiers. They are still there and now they are even building permanent structures in their camps. For the past three years they have been sending more weapons and food for their soldiers and built these permanent structures.

How can the Karen believe them? It doesn't look like they are planning on going anywhere from Karen areas. The concrete Burmese are building show that they don't plan on leaving.

"My duty is not finished even if I die. It's not finished until we win the revolution"

When I see the refugees and others who struggle I just want to work harder for revolution. I feel so sorry for my people when I see how poor they are and how hard they work… If the Karen had their own country, this wouldn't happen to them.

My duty is not finished even if I die. It's not finished until we win the revolution. I will not go back to live in Burma until the country is free.

x   x   x

" They [INGOs] Cannot Reach LAHU Areas and the Needs of the LAHU People "

Young Lahu Activist *Kyar Yin Shell*

Kyar Yin Shell is a 26-year-old young man from Kengtung, the 'dark and dirty' capital city of eastern Salween in the Shan State, where development is non-existent and electricity scarce. Kyar Yin Shell is Lahu, a little known ethnic group that lives scattered around the mountains of Burma, China, Laos, and Thailand. As most Lahu people, Kyar Yin Shell grew up in a village, but unlike many others he was lucky enough to go to school. As a teenager, hard-working Kyar Yin Shell had great hopes for his future until it all seems to end one day; wrong medical treatment left Kyar Yin Shell paralyzed. Kyar Yin Shell lost all hope for his future and like so many others in the Shan State, he became addicted to drugs. During those dark times, Kyar Yin Shell could never have known that he would not only survive and learn to live with his disability, but work actively for his people.

"My body cannot move, I am paralyzed"

My name is Kyar Yin Shell. I belong to Lahu ethnic group. Now I am 26 years old. I am from Kengtung, the capital city of eastern Salween. My parents are farmers. Most Lahu people are farmers. I have seven siblings, actually ten. Three already died before I was born. Five boys and five girls. Now seven of us are still alive.

When I was 14 years old, I became a disabled person because of wrong injection by a doctor in Burma. Without taking a test for malaria, the doctor injected me the malaria medicine. Then I don't remember... After that, 'my body cannot move. I am paralyzed.' They immediately sent me to the hospital to change my blood. My father, my mother and my sister were beside me. I don't know when they arrived. At that time I didn't go to school anymore.

I came back to my village and treated my leg with traditional medicine. But I couldn't walk very well so I didn't go to school anymore. I was so disappointed. I didn't have any hope to improve my education. In my dream at that time, I wanted to be an educated person. I was eager to learn. But from 2002 June to the beginning of 2005 there was no school for me. I didn't go to school.

At that time I didn't have any hope for my life. I was so disappointed with my life. So I started to use any drugs. My parents are farmers so during the day they went to the farm to grow rice. I stayed alone at home with no friends. So what I did was to start to smoke. I did it to find joy, but I couldn't find it.

At the time I used to smoke and also sometimes I used opium. Sometimes amphetamine. But I could not find any joy in my life at that time.

"The whole time I had no communication with my parents"

In 2005, I had a chance to go to Mae Sot to improve my education. My sister who called me [to study in Mae Sot] was working in Mae Tao clinic. I stayed in her house maybe for one week. After that she sent me to school [in Mae Pa].

I started to learn how to use a computer. In Kengtung when

I was in grade nine, in the timetable we had computer class. But we couldn't see the computer. We could see it in the room but nobody could go there. Because no light, no electricity. We could see it from outside the window but we couldn't touch it. Nobody touched it, not teachers, not anyone.

We just saw it, 'aaw computer looks like a TV.' During the computer class, we were playing in the class, talking to each other. It was like a break, no computer. When I was on grade nine there were almost 1,000 students but only ten computers. How can the students use them? Just only go and see them. But still I haven't heard that students have a chance to learn computers at the school.

I stayed at the school [in Mae Pa] for three or four years; from 2005 to 2008 until I passed grade ten. The whole time I had no communication with my parents... I went back in 2011. When my mother saw me she cried. They hadn't seen me and they hadn't heard anything. They didn't know anything about me. They thought they lost me.

"They don't know how to prevent pregnancy"

After graduating grade ten in Mae Sot, I started working with Lahu Youth Organization to participate in the movement. Then I had a chance to apply for a scholarship called Foreign Affairs

Training (FAT) in Chiang Mai. Fortunately I passed the entrance of the FAT. After I finished the FAT I had a chance to go to Malaysia for my internship, three months in Malaysia. Then I came back and joined the LDU, Lahu Democratic Union.

At the same time I was also working for my Lahu Youth Organization as an advocator to support the Lahu situation in Burma. As a part of the Lahu Youth Organization, I have conducted training inside Burma; democratic training and also training about reproductive health. When I went to conduct the training inside Burma, most Lahu people were very eager to learn about health, especially reproductive health. How to prevent HIV, how to prevent pregnancy, things like that. They didn't know.

I also I asked my mother, 'why did you have a lot of children?' She said to me, 'we didn't know how to prevent it.' It is normal in Lahu families. Some people have ten or fifteen children.

"There are a lot of armed groups in eastern Salween River"

In my village most people are Lahu but we also have Kachin and Akha. Shan village is a little bit far away from my village. Burmans are only temporary workers. Authorities are Lahu people. Just only police men and Burmese soldiers are Burmans. Around

Kyar Yin Shell giving family planning training for Lahu people in the Shan State.

my village the Burmese have a military camp. They are based around my village.

Lahu militia are not near my village but they are in other parts of Kengtung. There are a lot of armed groups in eastern Salween River. There's Wa, Shan, Lahu militia, Lahu BGF (Border Guard Force), also the SSA (Shan State Army). There are a lot of armed groups in Lahu areas.

Even though there is peace in some other areas in Burma,

not in Shan State. I am concerned about it. In eastern Shan State they have a lot of armed groups. They don't have proper communication and they are separate. Sometimes they have misunderstandings.

In the golden triangle there's also very famous production of drugs. Last time I went to visit the Lahu area, I saw the Lahu young people, their skin color is changing. Like yellow or brown, because they use a lot of drugs. We have this kind of situation, especially around the border. Drug abuse is a big problem for Lahu youth. In some areas they can find it very easily, they can use drugs very easily, opium.

"I don't blame them [INGOs] but they cannot reach Lahu areas"

There's no development [in Lahu areas]. Nothing has changed. Since I was a child nothing has changed, it's the same. The town of Kengtung is very old, very dirty. No new buildings. When I was a child Tachilek was a small town, I mean the border town, now it is bigger. There has been some development. But not in Kengtung, sorry still no internet, still dark. No electricity. Sometimes the light comes, sometimes not.

Some Lahu villages don't have schools, no teachers. Especially in the Wa area near the China-Burma border. At schools in Lahu areas, they don't teach Lahu language, just only Burmese. They don't have a chance to study Lahu. They are not allowed to teach it.

[I want to] set up one civil society organisation in my hometown, to work for the development of Lahu areas. [Currently] there are just only INGOs like World Vision, something like that. Actually I don't blame them but they cannot reach Lahu areas and the needs of the Lahu people. They don't know about it. Because they also cooperate with the government, they follow the laws of the government.

x   x   x

In 2014 and 2015, Kyar Yin Shell had a chance to participate in the Liberty and Leadership Forum, which is supported and organised by George W. Bush and his George W. Bush Institute in the U.S.

Today, Kyar Yin Shell continues working for Lahu Youth Organization and Lahu Democratic Union to support the Lahu situation and give awareness about family planning and democracy in rural Shan State.

Kyar Yin Shell also hopes to work towards eliminating drugs from his homeland.

" Our Village Was Burnt "

Karen Refugee *Naw Woo*

Naw Woo doesn't know her age exactly but she thinks that she is about 40 years old. Naw Woo grew up in a small village in the Karen State, helping her parents make a living with hill-side plantations. Conditions were harsh and sometimes the villagers had little more to eat than rice with salt. Other times they had to substitute rice for bamboo shoot or anything else they could find in the jungle. The villagers also regularly fled from Burmese soldiers who came to their village with no warning, demanding porters and torturing and beating anyone who got caught running away from them. Naw Woo and other villagers lived in a constant state of fear, and many villagers lost their lives amidst fighting between Burmese and Karen soldiers. Eventually, Burmese soldiers burnt their whole village to the ground. Naw Woo now lives in Mae La refugee camp, the largest of the camps on the Thailand-Burma border, and hopes she will not have to go back to the land she so desperately escaped from.

"Normally we ate what we could find in the jungle"

Naw Woo comes from Haw Thaw Khee village, near Hlaing Bwe Township in the Karen State. The villagers were poor and Naw Woo's family survived by cultivating rice and vegetables on hill-side farms. Some years were luckier than others, and although Naw Woo and her family would normally eat two or three times a day, sometimes they only had enough for one meal.

When I was in my village, which is in Burma, I struggled a lot for my family's livelihood. We grew crops but it was not enough for my family. So, we went to the forest and found some vegetables that we could eat. We didn't have any good jobs. We didn't have enough food to eat but we could manage it. We ate rice every day, with chilli and salt. Sometimes we didn't have chilli so we ate just rice with salt.

When we were cultivating the land, we had to burn the land first. Then we would start planting. If we were lucky the land was fertile and we got a good result... But sometimes when you burn the land, and it doesn't burn very well, you can't get very much rice. And then if you can't get much rice, you cannot eat much for the next year. Then we went to the jungle and got bamboo shoot, and would just eat it as rice. We boiled the shoot and ate it instead of rice.

Sometimes we ate special food like chicken. Maybe once every week or two weeks. Normally we ate what we could find in the jungle, like different plants, leaves and bamboo shoot.

In the village everyone works and the children help their parents in the farms. I never went to school. There is no school in the village, so no children in the village go to school.

Naw Woo explains that her family couldn't afford to buy blankets, and they would sleep around a fire to try to stay warm.

Because I couldn't afford to buy a blanket, I had to use the fire as a blanket.

"We were afraid and scared of the troops. The villagers lived in fear"

I had a lot of difficulties living in the village… Burmese troops usually came two or three times every year. The troops camped near the village every time they arrived. And they used the villagers to build their camp and buildings. They asked villagers to be porters.

If anyone didn't want to do it and ran away or hid somewhere then they asked the village chief to call them back. The soldiers also chased the villagers but most of the villagers didn't come back until the troops left. If they caught any of the villagers they tortured or beat them.

When the troops came they just appeared, nobody knew they would come in advance. We were afraid and scared of the troops. The villagers lived in fear.

Burmese soldiers came to our house many times, at least three times. My husband also had to go for porter sometimes… When he went for portering, it usually took about one week. DKBA (Democratic Karen Benevolent Army – a splinter group from the Karen National Union that at the time sided with the Burma Army) also came sometimes, but DKBA soldiers were nicer than Burmese soldiers. DKBA soldiers are Karen and understand Karen and they even talked to the villagers in a friendlier way. But we were afraid of both.

"Our village was burnt"

There was a lot of fighting between the KNU and Burmese or DKBA soldiers near Naw Woo's village. She explains that although the soldiers didn't seem to intentionally shoot at the villagers, some villagers died because of the fighting.

Some people hid under their houses making a hole in the ground. There was one woman breastfeeding her baby who came out from the hole and was hit by a bullet and died.

One of my relatives was shot because he was accused of being a KNU soldier. Burmese soldiers also shot towards one house as they thought KNU soldiers were hiding there, but instead two young brothers and one sister who were hiding in the house died.

Yes, sometimes they fought around our houses in our village. Then, our houses were shot at and our village was burned. And some of the villagers were killed. There was a pregnant woman who was shot and [who] died.

"We tried to avoid places that might have landmines or Burmese soldiers"

After years of abuse and fear, Naw Woo and her family couldn't stand the situation and, given the opportunity, fled to the Thailand-Burma border. Naw Woo, her husband and their three children travelled across the jungle on foot, following other people who knew the way to Thailand.

My friends told me about the camp and that we should go to Mae la. If we lived in Mae La, we wouldn't need to be afraid of anything. We will be safe from the danger of Burmese military. We don't also need to worry about accommodation and livelihood. We will get support. If we go to another place we would face many problems. If we continue to live in Burma, we will always need to be afraid or frightened.

[When we fled] it was the rainy season. The Burmese [military] came to our house at that time. We were afraid of them and we fled from the house. On the way we walked, we had to be afraid of the landmines. We just followed other people.

I came with about 30 people. Some stepped on a landmine and died. I saw two boys and one girl stepped on the landmine and died. We walked with fear and we could go through the forest and we got to the border.

We can say that we were so lucky at that time. That's why we escaped from the danger and we got to a safe place. When we got to Thailand side, we were less afraid. We were just afraid on Burma side.

"In the camp, I am not cold"

I like to live in the camp, a lot more than in the village before. In the camp, I am not cold. I have a blanket because they [The Border Consortium] gave me a blanket. Our house in Mae La is better than the one we had in Burma. I like living in Mae La, I like the house. The best thing about living in Mae La is that I can eat, wear clothes, and my children can go to school. There are a lot of good things about living here.

Since I arrived, I have never left the camp. I don't go anywhere. The only place I go to is to get the food ration inside the camp. I have never gone back to Burma. Since I have arrived here, I have never gone back to Burma.

Although Naw Woo's family get rations in the camp, her husband does daily work for additional income.

He [Naw Woo's husband] does any work he can get for a daily wage… Usually in the corn fields. We get some money like that. He works on different corn fields, sometimes close to the camp

View of Mae La camp, the largest of the Thai border refugee camps with over 40,000 refugees.

and other times far away. They [her husband and other refugees] just work as much as they can. Sometimes he might stay away for weeks if there is work. Then he comes back with some money. He is not allowed to leave the camp, it is illegal to go outside so he has to try to find a way to go around the Thai checkpoints. A lot of people know ways around the checkpoints through the jungle. But they are afraid to do that. They are scared of the Thai soldiers.

[My husband works] because we need some food and candles for our children. If not, my children won't be able to use candles to get light at night for their studying.

"I am worried about repatriation"

Naw Woo says that if the camp is closed, she wants to live in Thailand. She is not registered with the United Nations High Commissioner for Refugees (UNHCR) and is thus ineligible for resettlement to a third country.

If possible I want to live in Thailand and not go back to Burma. But I think it's impossible. If I was registered [with the UNHCR], and had a chance to go to a third country, I would go. I don't want to go back to Burma. I've had enough of living in Burma. I am sick of living there. I don't have relatives in Burma because my parents have already died. But my friends are still there in Burma... I have no contact with them, there is no way to contact people in Burma. I cannot buy a mobile phone.

The policy of the camp is getting stricter than before. For example, before, we were allowed to go outside of the camp but now we are not allowed. It is a problem for some people. Some people said they feel like they are living in a cage. They are suffocating [because] of living in the camp.

Before we got enough rations but now we don't. Rice is still enough for us now but oil and fish paste are not enough. And we are allowed to use candles just until 9 pm. After that, we are not allowed. If we break that rule, we will be taken to a jail for a few days and our rations will be cut.

I am worried about repatriation because, it is ok if the situation in Burma is getting better and safer for us. If not, I am afraid to go back. If everything in Burma is going well, yes I dare to go back. Another thing I worry about is accommodation for us. If we don't have house to live and job to earn money, there is no way for me to go back to Burma. When we live in Burma, if we don't have money, we all will starve and die.

In the future, I want my children go to university and I want them to be successful. As for me, I am getting old, I will just stay at home and look after them. The most important is the education for my children.

x   x   x

Unlike before, Naw Woo's family is currently unable to earn additional income through daily work outside the camp. Whilst surviving in the camps is becoming more and more difficult, rumours of repatriation are sweeping through refugee communities, causing fear and anxiety among the refugees who do not feel safe to return.

Indeed, the situation on the ground in Burma indicates increased militarisation, ongoing human rights violations, and fragile ceasefires.

Refugees like Naw Woo and her family should have a right to return of their own free will and in their own time, with a sense of dignity and hope.

" I Was the ONLY WOMAN among the Men "

Leader of the Guerrilla *Saw Mra Raza Linn*

Saw Mra Raza Linn is the founder and Chairperson of Rakhine Women's Union and a founding member of Women's League of Burma. During the democracy uprising in Burma in 1988, Mra Raza Linn led thousands of people in pro-democracy marches in her native Rakhine State. She conducted nonviolent protests against local government officials and travelled extensively to promote the inclusion of diverse religious groups in Burma's democracy movement.

Mra Raza Linn also worked hard to address ongoing violence against women and to release many local political prisoners from jail. When Martial Law was declared in Burma in September 1988, the government ordered the capture of Mra Raza Linn and like many other prominent democracy leaders, she was forced to flee the country. Mra Raza Linn fled to the deep jungles of Bangladesh, where she soon became a leader of the armed guerrilla struggle, before resuming her political activism on behalf of Rakhine women and children. Saw Mra Raza Linn continues to work for national reconciliation, peace and for advancing women's participation in all spheres of decision making level for establishing a democratic and peaceful country.

1988 – If you want to continue the struggle, follow me!

In 1988 I was one of the active leaders of the democracy movement in the Rakhine [Arakan] State. At that time I was a teacher. So I organized many people and delivered my first democracy speech at Wangabar Ground in Sittwe on 9th of August, 1988. But the government was very angry with me. On 21st of August we seized all government offices in my native town, Rathedaung, without any bloodshed. The government was angry and wanted to kill me. In 1988, September 18, they seized state power. At that time I was at Rathedaung, running the office and controlling my township. After they seized state power, many gun men came in the township and then they searched for me to kill me. They shouted: I want to kill Mra Raza Linn, putting the gun through her mouth! Something like that. They were shouting everywhere.

Thousands and thousands of people, they were following me before the government seized state power. They all disappeared. There were only about ten or twelve people around me. So I thought at that time that if I want to continue my struggle I should not stay in Burma. I should go somewhere... So I decided to leave my native country and took shelter on the Bangladesh-Burma border... After they seized the power I told my colleagues I must leave my country. If you want to continue the struggle, follow me! I called them. So eleven men they followed with me. And then we crossed the Bay of Bengal with a small engine boat, and took shelter on the Bangladesh-Burma border. All of us became soldiers, eleven men together with me. All became soldiers.

Kill me!
I don't want to call my daughter to come back

When I was away, the people were very much afraid for me. But my parents, they tried to meet me. When I left my parents, they were very old. But I couldn't carry them together with me. So they were left behind. And then they tried and tried to meet me. Some people sympathized with me and my parents. Among them, Mr. Kyaw Thein from Buthidaung sympathized with us very much. Mr. Kyaw Thein came to the jungle and searched for me and called me back to Rakhine State to live with my parents. Oh no, I denied. Impossible to go back without getting democracy. I will stay on the Bangladesh border until successful democracy movement, I replied to him.

My father was very old, and they had not enough money, not enough food to eat. They faced a lot of problems. The government arrested my parents and put them in Buthidaung jail three times. My father was suffering fever a lot. The local government sent me a letter, your father is very sick, you come back. They put my father in Buthidaung jail and they tricked me like that many times. My father said: Kill me! I don't want to call my daughter to come back. My father was against them.

Woman leading the armed struggle

Before going to Bangladesh, I was thinking like maybe there are many men like a big army. But my thinking was not accurate. Not so much a big army, they have not enough arms, they have not enough food to eat. They have very much difficulty for survival. I came to know the practical life of revolution after I arrived to the revolutionary area.

I faced a lot of difficulties in the jungle. Without enough food, blankets. Suffering malaria. About two years and six months I was in the jungle with ALP [Arakan Liberation Party] and another alliance at that time; NUFA, National United Front of Arakan. I joined them, and within three months I became high rank position as a leader of the National United Front of Arakan. I became one of the leaders with the armed struggle.

I was the only woman among the men. In the evening time, I was very much home sick, for my parents. And then, my friends, and then, my country. On the hill, in the small barrack, I was alone thinking, dreaming:

Aww if there were one of the big women armies, with wearing a uniform, if they would come out. I would be happy.

I was thinking like that. I was sitting on the hill like that every evening. Other people they were enjoying talking and telling stories or something. They had a group. They took care of me how they could. But I felt as if I was alone... And then I saw monkey family, the monkey family became my company. In the evening the monkey family was happily enjoying themselves near my hut. And I had a dog. The dog was very intelligent.

I was the only woman there, in the alliance... Sometimes I

was sick. When I was suffering fever, I wanted to drink water, but sometimes there was no one near me. And I couldn't go anywhere. Sometimes I faced a lot of difficulties. The party also ordered that no one was allowed to go to a woman's hut for my safety. So nobody could come except health care workers. They were also busy with other patients.

At that time I faced a lot of problems, a lot of suffering. Sometimes not enough food to eat and not enough blankets for sleeping. I slept with a fire, a bonfire. I collected firewood, big firewood during the day and then before sleeping I made a fire near me. This side already hot and this side cold. A lot of problems.

Revolutionary life is very difficult. Most people cannot resist long in the revolution. The Alliance was broken in 1991. We had five important leaders remaining in the alliance (National United Front of Arakan). And the others, around seven comrades, they were left with me. Other people had already gone, already gone away. Among the five leaders, I remained. I didn't want to go away. I wanted to be there. With a gun.

I was thinking I want to see many women here. Always I was thinking like that, I want to see many women to come out, working for freedom. Freedom means the self-determination of my country, of my Rakhine Pray (State) and Rakhine people. So I wanted to found a women army. At that time, I was thinking, aww women army, and women organisation.

A women's organisation must be needed

I tried to found RWU in 1990. I tried but many people were not encouraging me to found it. Slowly and slowly I tried. Many people opposed me not to found. But in 1995 there was a world conference, a women's conference held in Beijing. That conference encouraged me more to found the RWU, because there in Beijing conference I met about 35,000 women from all over the world.

They talked about women. They talked about gender equality. They talked about becoming the brilliant women in the world. They talked about women's participation at the decision-making level.

That conference encouraged me a lot. I got a lot of energy, mental energy to found the Rakhine Women's Union. And then without giving up, I tried again after 1995. And then on November 4 in 1998, I established the RWU, Rakhine Women's Union, on the Bangladesh-Burma border.

About 60% of population of Rakhine State is women. Most of the women are uneducated. Most of them don't know how to survive in their life, how to protect their life, how to protect their Rakhine State, or how to try development for them. So I want to give education to the women first, I want to have many qualified

women to work for my country, and to work for my people. That is the main reason for RWU.

Another reason is that when making a decision in NUFA, I was only woman, so there were very few votes on my side. Men were on one side and they won. So I thought I need a lot more women to reach my aims. I was thinking for a better solution, but they [men] don't know, they don't understand a woman's thinking. So I thought that a women organisation must be needed. In 1998, after spending about 10 years I could found the RWU, Rakhine Women's Union.

After 24 years I came back to my country

After 24 years in exile, the government allowed me to go back to Burma After getting the ceasefire agreement with the ALP, Arakan Liberation Party, they allowed me to go back. The party also allowed me to open the Kyauktaw liaison office. Unfortunately between June and July 2012, a big problem was breaking out in Rakhine State. Muslim and Rakhine community were clashing and many people became homeless. At that time the government re-thought not to allow me in that situation to come back to the country. I tried and tried many times. At last the government allowed me to come back to Burma but just as a very low profile person.

When I returned back to my Rakhine State, I thought that there will be about 50 people receiving me on the sea port because 144 order was issued in Rakhine State [unlawful assembly of more than five or six people]. But it was a big surprise that there were many people welcoming me at the sea port. So I was very happy and couldn't stop crying... I couldn't say anything; I couldn't control myself because I was very homesick missing my people for a long time. When I crossed the Nef River from Bangladesh side, I could control, I was happy and I thought that I am very lucky. But when an interview with news channel at the Sittwe Sea Port came, I couldn't control myself. I cried.

When I saw my country, it was very different from other countries and people were very poor. It was worse than I expected. However, I felt that I am very much lucky; I can get a chance to see my country and to see my people, hopefully I might be able to work for my people and country.

After a week, I visited my native Aung Sike village in Rathedaung Township, I didn't see nearly half of the people from my village that I knew. The rest of the people and the new generation were already expecting to see me after 24 years coming back to my country. When I reached my village, aww nearly the whole village and all villagers were crying with happiness and sorrow.

The youngest one became a guerrilla

When I was young, there were three students from my village who were studying together in Sittwe, the capital of Rakhine State. I was the youngest girl among those three. I was class 5, twelve years old, the second one was class 8, and the eldest was class 10. When the three of us grew up, one became a doctor, one became an army officer and the youngest girl became a teacher. Before 1988, we lost contact with each other because we were serving respective duties in our respective places.

Nowadays it is very interesting, as one of us became an MP in the Burma parliament, and he is very famous. One of us became a Captain in the [Burmese] army, now retired. And I became a guerrilla leader. After more than 24 years, we met again in

Mra Raza Linn crossing the jungle with men from the ALP.

Naypyidaw, the new capital of Burma, when I came for peace talks with the government. Everyone was happy, and wanted to see each other. Aww what happened to our life… The youngest one became a guerrilla woman.

In 2000, I became the joint general secretary of ALP (Arakan Liberation Party) and in 2012, I became the general secretary. The life of a revolutionary woman is not easy, living in the jungle with male friends, working together with them, and taking heavy responsibility.

I have to cross many mountains to arrive to ALP headquarters. I stay on the way two nights and two days crossing the very high mountains. This is my life… I have also faced a lot of difficulties in life. Sometimes I have a chance to stay in a standard hotel in another country for advocacy work for Burma's democracy movement.

Now I am working as an executive member of ALP, the Chairperson of Rakhine Women's Union, a founding member of Women's League of Burma, and working actively as a member of NCCT (Nationwide Ceasefire Coordinating Team).

"If we speak alone, the men in the movement will never listen to us. If we gather together, we can make them listen"

Acknowledgments

First and foremost, we are extremely grateful to the interviewees for their courage to share openly about their life stories with Burma Link. We are also grateful to all Burma Link volunteers and interns who helped make this happen, especially all the people from Burma who volunteered their time to translate and transcribe many of these stories.

We would also like to thank everyone who participated in the crowdfunding campaign to make this book possible - it is with those funds that we were able to publish this book. Burma Link is also grateful to the three individuals who played a central role in this project; Leena (co-founder of Burma Link), Atun (co-founder of Burma Link), and Nay Satkyar Naing (Burmese editor and advisor).

Finally, we wish to thank everyone who has been involved in the process in one way or another - this book would not have been possible without the help and support of many individuals across the world.

x   x   x

Methodology

The stories in this book were collected by Burma Link through qualitative life story interviews between 2013 and 2015. Burma Link chose specific stories for the book based on the impact each story had on us while also considering the diversity of ethnicities and background.

All the interviewers were well aware of local customs and cultures. The interviews were conducted in a highly flexible manner, and interviewers adapted their questions depending on what the person was talking about. Guiding questions about important life events and experiences were used as a rough guideline only. The purpose was simply to understand the interviewees' lives and give them a chance to share and voice their experiences and feelings in a safe and respectful setting.

The interviewees' concerns were put above all else and we made sure the interviewees were completely satisfied with the information used. Whenever possible, we also let the interviewees fact check everything in their stories and ensure everything is written as they want it to be.

The interviews for the stories included in this book were conducted in and around Chiang Mai and Mae Sot as well as in Mae La refugee camp and a Karen army camp inside the Karen State. The interviews mostly took place in private and quiet settings where the interviewees felt most comfortable, such as their home or workplace.

Most of the interviews included in this book were conducted in English. Other languages used included Burmese, Karen, and Tavoy. Care was taken to retain both the original voice and meaning in translations.

All interviewees made an informed decision to take part. They were explained the reasons for conducting the interview, and they were told about Burma Link's objective to project their voices to, and share their stories with, a domestic and international audience.

It was made clear that interviewees can answer only what they want to answer, and can say if they want to leave anything out of the transcript. All the interviewees were given the right to remain anonymous and only talk about things that they were comfortable sharing and talking about. Care was taken to only use the identity information that the interviewee was comfortable sharing, and we never started recording without asking the person first.

All the interviewees who we are able to reach will receive a copy of this book in English and Burmese, and their feedback will be welcomed and encouraged. Burma Link did its very best to ensure the people feel empowered, happy and proud to share their stories during and after the interview process.

The stories in this book are not meant to represent the Voices for Change on the Thailand-Burma border, but they are nevertheless invaluable in shedding some insight into the struggles of those who have experienced the conflict in Burma first-hand.

x   x   x

I don't feel REGRET

I don't feel HURT

I have done what I think was RIGHT

Soe Lwin

Former Teenage Political Prisoner

www.ingramcontent.com/pod-product-compliance
Lightning Source LLC
Chambersburg PA
CBHW050500080326
40788CB00001B/3918